# The WRIGHT EXPERIENCE

# The WRIGHT EXPERIENCE
## A Master Architect's Vision

Sara Hunt ▣ Introduction by ▣ With photographs by
Editor ▣ Margo Stipe ▣ Balthazar Korab

Saraband

Published by Saraband (Scotland) Ltd.
T/L, 61 Peel Street
Glasgow G11 5LX, Scotland
hermes@saraband.net
www.saraband.net

Editor: Sara Hunt
Introduction: Margo Stipe
Contributors: Doreen Ehrlich, Jessica Hodge,
and Robin Langley Sommer
Design and illustration: Deborah Hayes
Associate editor: Clare Haworth-Maden
Editorial reader: Kathryn Smith
Digital mastering of images: Christian Korab

ISBN: 978-1-887354-60-8

Printed and bound in China

1  3  5  7  9  10  8  6  4  2

Page 1 & 3 photographs: Detail of the studio/gallery at the Susan
Lawrence Dana House, Springfield, Illinois. Page 2: An interior at the
_____ Bartlesville, Oklahoma. Opposite: The Gregor Affleck
_____ oomfield Hills, Michigan. (© Balthazar Korab)

FOR KEITH HUNT

# CONTENTS
▣ ▣ ▣ ▣ ▣ ▣

# INTRODUCTION

□ □ □ □ □ □ □ □ □ □ □ □

"In some of Frank Lloyd Wright's buildings it is hard to tell where nature stops and man begins. The truth is that nature is present in these buildings as much as it is in the flow of a waterfall, the growth of a plant and the rock formation of a mountain glen."

—*John de Koven Hill, 1955*

Great architecture is magical and transformational; it engages the keen observer on all levels because it harmoniously unites the human spirit with the natural world through the built environment. Great architects are magicians and very rare, but as the designer of dozens of iconic buildings, Frank Lloyd Wright easily ranks among the most gifted. His built works and unbuilt designs have inspired and influenced, amazed, bewildered, and delighted generations of architects, homeowners, scholars, and students. Dozens of exhibits have been mounted and hundreds of books and thousands of articles have been written about Wright and his work from a dizzying range of perspectives—all reaffirming Wright's indelible contribution to not only architectural history, but the patterns of American lives.

Wright's career lasted for seven decades, during which his buildings changed as the social environment changed—from the formalities of the dress and manners of the early 1900s to the ever more casual living of the post-World War II era. But while the forms changed, his architectural principles and the grammar of his designs remained consistent. He identified his architecture as "organic"—as that which grows as natural forms grow—and he defined it as that which "proceeds, persists, creates, according to the nature of man and his circumstances as they both *change*." Convinced of the rightness—and even the morality—of his cause, and armed with very definite ideas about what constituted good architecture, Wright uncompromisingly preached the gospel of the "organic" through his buildings, writings, and lectures.

In the decades since his death, Wright's work has increasingly captured the attention of the international community, while in the United States, his work is being re-evaluated in terms of the lessons that it might offer for the future. Clearly of ongoing interest, what exactly is it that makes Wright's work so attractive?

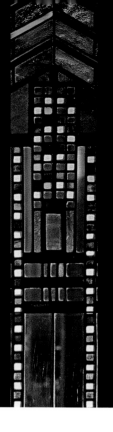

Fallingwater, the house for Edgar J. Kaufmann, Sr., Bear Run, Pennsylvania (opposite, below), and an entrance gate to Taliesin, Wisconsin (opposite, above). Wright designed more than 250 art-glass windows (left), doors, and light panels for the Susan Lawrence Dana House. The enclosed terrace of the Isabel Roberts House in River Forest, Illinois (right), has been altered several times to accommodate the growth of the British elm tree that rises through the roof.

Wright's clients—and later owners of Wright houses—have often spoken of how much they love their houses; of how beautiful they are; and of how, by simply living in the house, they have become attuned to the constantly changing manifestations of the natural world around them. By reuniting the interior of the human shelter with the natural environment outside through sight lines within and without the building, and in the twisting paths of movement, the changing perspectives, and the angles of repose, new experiences and patterns were created and everyday life enriched. The key to this successful marriage, and the consequent magic of Wright's architecture, I believe, is found in understanding his view of nature.

Wright's long life (1867–1959) spanned decades of two centuries. Much of his youth was spent among his mother's family, the remarkable Lloyd-Jones clan, in the Wisconsin valley where Wright himself would later build Taliesin. Farmers, teachers, and preachers, they were dedicated Unitarians and well versed in the writings of the Transcendentalists, which made much of man's proper place in nature being to live in harmony with it. While Wright took full advantage of the material opportunities presented by the unprecedented scientific and technological advances of the twentieth century, he never lost sight of the nineteenth-century Emersonian spiritual and romantic values with which he had grown up, including a reverence for nature that guided not only his spiritual life, but his architecture.

Over one hundred years ago, Wright bemoaned the disconnect between humanity and nature and what he saw as the related division between the secular and sacred. For him matter and spirit were inseparable. Having grown up close to the land, nature gave Wright both faith in the underlying order of the world as we experience it and constant inspiration for his architecture. Nature was his church and his muse, and his architecture reflects this close association. He chose to spell nature with a capital "N", believed

Nature was all of the body of God that we will ever see, and that to be divorced from it and its beauty greatly diminishes the quality of our lives. He wanted to re-establish that connection, and was convinced changing how we live, and realigning our lives with respect to the greater world of nature was one way of doing that. Human beings, in this view, are but one aspect of the vast, cosmic reality; the larger world of Nature is one organic whole, the well-being of that whole being dependent on the well-being and cooperation of its parts. Like wind, like rocks, like water, like all other living forms, every aspect of Nature shares the same energy to which it owes its existence. "I can only regard the visible world as supreme artistry, eternally developing, in which inheres this principle of organic integrity and laws of inherent unity," he wrote, in *The Print and the Renaissance* (1917). Humankind, then, has the duty and responsibility of being respectful to the rest of the cosmic community.

Wright sought to refocus the way in which we look at building and to re-establish architecture as the "mother art." In the process he hoped to reintroduce poetry into the art of building in order to shelter not only the physical being, but the human spirit in the harmony and quietude required to keep it nourished and inspired. In a talk given to the Taliesin Fellowship in 1952, Wright expanded on his ideal of an architecture that was in harmony with nature:

*I think fundamentally the Mother Art is here ready now to go to work to persuade humanity that the basis of all culture and essential to it is this matter of building yourself into a harmonious environment. Harmonious with nature wherever you are. Not to insult the site, not to outrage the elements of beauty to which you are born and in which you yourself should be beautiful too, of course, but if beauty is the highest and finest kind of morality, and I believe it is, there is your religion. There is where your center of life should be strong.*

To realize materially such a spiritual end, Wright created environments of simplicity and repose through carefully composed plans and elevations based on a consistent, geometric grammar while paying careful attention to the nature of the materials used and skillfully implementing the integration of the building with the site. As an advocate of beauty, order, and harmony in both architecture and life, Wright sought to integrate all three in every building that he designed, recomposing the natural materials of the area into a structure that would complement and intensify the beauty of the site. The end result of this was a revolutionary reworking of architectural space that has long been credited with changing how we live. Through simplification of form, line, and color, and through the poise, balance, and rhythmic play of parts, Wright created plastic, fluent, and coherent spaces that enhance the changing physical and spiritual life of the people who live in them by insisting on their interaction with the natural world surrounding them.

That there is a critical need to join in such a communion with nature is at the core of Wright's architectural philosophy. For him, the means of achieving the objective of housing the human spirit in worthy fashion demands the deepest involvement of nature—whether in the form of outward, nature-seeking houses or inward, reflective places of worship—so that the resulting building will grow and harmonize with its surroundings in much the same organic fashion as a living tree.

Although uncompromisingly modern, Wright's buildings are simultaneously timeless creations that grow in their places like idealized patterns of their landscapes. In a world increasingly, and precariously, out of balance due largely to the unprecedented human assault on nature in our attempt to bend it to our will—and the consequent wounding of the Earth's community of life that should be humankind's partner in this cosmic adventure—Wright's buildings attract us as beacons of light and comforting refuges from the disquieting maelstrom that swirls around us. As a visionary driven by dreams of an organic harmony on Earth, Wright's wizardry continues to soothe and inspire.

In 1953, writing several years before his death in 1959, Wright gave this insightful evaluation of his work:

*I know well that my buildings see clearly not only the color, drift and inclination of my own day but feed its spirit. All of them seek to provide forms adequate to integrate and harmonize our new materials, tools and shapes with the democratic life-ideal of my own day and time. Thus do I know work that is for all time.*

The Roland Reisley House (above) appears to grow organically out of its leafy hillside setting in the cooperative utopian community of Usonia, near Pleasantville, New York. In this space (below) at the 1948 house for Herman T. Mossberg, we see Wright's fluency with ordered, geometric lines resulting in a rhythmic, harmonious design that integrates the interior levels.

Margo Stipe
Taliesin West, Scottsdale, Arizona, 2008

## Illustrated Timeline of
# Frank Lloyd Wright's
## Life and Work

*Pictured at right: Wright's studio in Oak Park; the Japanese Pavilion under construction at Chicago's World Fair, 1893 (far right).*

**Note:** The chronology of built projects and selected events in Frank Lloyd Wright's life presented in this timeline is based largely on information published by the Frank Lloyd Wright Foundation. The dates given for buildings refer to Wright's design concept, rather than construction. Sources (including Wright's own written works) from which this data was drawn do not always agree on dates, especially for buildings designed before 1932, so that dates given here may vary from those in other publications. Key events in Wright's life and career are listed in the upper portion of the timeline. The lower section provides a list of all his built works (he also designed a similar number of unrealized projects). Further analysis or context is given in the highlighted panels.

**1867** Born on June 8, in Richland Center, Wis., to William Cary Wright and Anna Lloyd Jones Wright.

**1878** Moves with his family to Madison, Wis. Starts a custom, which continues into the 1880s, of spending summers at the James Lloyd Jones farm near Spring Green, Wis.

**1885** Wright's parents divorce.

**1886** Attends the University of Wisconsin.

**1887** Moves from Madison, Wis., to Chicago, Ill.

**1889** Marries Catherine Lee Tobin.

**1890** Assigned all residential design work for Adler and Sullivan. A first child, Lloyd, is born.

**1893** Establishes his own practice at his home and studio in Oak Park, Ill.

**1894** A daughter, Catherine, is born.

**1895** A son, David Samuel, is born.

**1896** Writes "Architecture, Architect, and Client," a lecture, and "Work Song," a credo.

**1897** Moves office to Steinway Hall, Chicago, Ill.

**1898** A daughter, Frances, is born.

---

## 1865 • 1880 • 1890 • 1895

---

While **Wright's distinctive career began** with his work for Louis Sullivan, his aesthetic and certainty of mission were partly born of the essential DNA of his family. Common throughout the close-knit dynasty that got its U.S. start in the lush valley of Spring Green, Wisconsin, when his grandparents emigrated from south Wales in 1844, was an unshakable sense of purpose and passion for life.

Dedicated Unitarians, they lived their motto, "Truth Against the World." It was into this group of farmers and ministers that Wright was born in 1867. His father, William Cary Wright, though a Baptist minister, was more an outsider for his uncertain work ethic and emotional distance. His deep love of music, however, would resonate forever with the nascent architect. His mother, Anna Lloyd Jones, is often credited as having a seer's sense of Wright's future. Imbuing in him a love for Emerson and Thoreau, she was also quick to recognize his precocious talents.

The young family settled for periods in New England; Wright, however, returned to work his Uncle James's fertile farm for most summers of his childhood. Here he came to embrace the Unitarian belief in "harmony between spiritual and earthly realms" that would define his work in years to come. At least as influential was the Froebel training system (the "gifts") introduced to nine-year-old Frank by the determined Anna. Wright's experience with the wooden shapes and the system's visual and tactile exercises would later be considered intrinsic to his exquisite built geometries.

Leaving home in 1886 to embark on engineering studies in Madison, Wright's first projects would soon reveal this deeply personal mix of influence and natural talent.

**1885** Part-time job as draftsman with Allan D. Conover, University of Wisconsin engineering professor.

**1886** Involved in building **Unity Chapel** (near Spring Green, Wis.) for Lloyd Jones family.

**1887–89** Employed in Chicago by Joseph L. Silsbee, then Adler and Sullivan; played role in design of original **Hillside Home School Building** (near Spring Green, Wis., demolished), credited to Silsbee, but claimed by Wright.

**1889** Designed own **home and studio** (Oak Park, Ill.).

Joseph Lyman Silsbee, a Chicago architect whom Wright first encountered when his uncle Jenkin commissioned a design for a small chapel, hired Wright at $8 per week as a tracer. But within a year, in 1889, Wright had obtained a coveted place with the recently established firm of Adler and Sullivan. His position there was fraught, just as it was protected: he was much favored by partner **Louis H. Sullivan**, the revolutionary modernist and proponent of design with purpose. Reviling the prevalent Classicism and Beaux Arts style, the American architectural sea change that Sullivan championed would eventually become known as the Chicago School.

Sullivan soon made Wright his assistant, both lending the newlywed money to build his own home and, by 1890, passing on all the residential work that the firm contracted. In thrall to the man he would always refer to as "*lieber Meister*," Wright took Sullivan's idiom farther and rapidly developed his own vocabulary, applying it to the remarkable range of homes that sprang up in Oak Park to his innovative, gorgeously detailed specifications.

**1890** Houses for **James Charnley** (Ocean Springs, Miss.) and **W.S. MacHarg** (Chicago, Ill.); cottage and stable for **Louis H. Sullivan** (Ocean Springs, Miss.).

**1891** House for **James Charnley** (Chicago, Ill.).

**1892** Houses for **Thomas Gale** and **Robert Parker** (both Oak Park, Ill.), **George Blossom** (Chicago, Ill.), **W. Irving Clark** and **Robert Emmond** (both La Grange, Ill.), **Dr. Allison Harlan** and **Albert Sullivan** (both Chicago, Ill., both demolished).

**1893** Houses for **Walter Gale** and **Francis Wooley** (both Oak Park, Ill.); house and stables for **William H. Winslow** (River Forest, Ill.); cottage for **Robert Lamp** and Lake Mendota Boathouse (both Madison, Wis., both demolished); **playhouse** added to own Oak Park, Ill., residence.

**1894** Houses for **Frederick Bagley** (Hinsdale, Ill.) and **Peter Goan** (La Grange, Ill.); house remodeled for **Dr. H.W. Bassett** (Oak Park, Ill., demolished); four houses for **Robert Roloson** (Chicago, Ill.).

The Chicago that Wright arrived in was a hotbed of construction following the 1871 fire. By the time of the **World's Columbian Exposition** in 1893, the city was at the forefront of American architecture, thanks to Louis Sullivan and his groundbreaking Auditorium Building project.

The exposition (or World's Fair), which astounded visitors with its incandescent lighting, was architecturally a Classicist rout. As conceived by Daniel Burnham, the site was a showcase for the Beaux Arts movement; only the international pavilions and Sullivan's transportation center represented other possibilities.

**1895** Francis Apartments for Terre Haute Trust Company and Edward C. Waller Apartments (both Chicago, Ill., both demolished); Francisco Terrace Apartments for Edward C. Waller (Chicago, Ill.); houses for Chauncey Williams (River Forest, Ill.) and Nathan G. Moore (Oak Park, Ill.); house remodeled for H.P. Young (Oak Park, Ill.).

**1896** Houses for **H.C. Goodrich** and **George Smith** (both Oak Park, Ill.) and **Isidore Heller** (Chicago, Ill.); house remodeled and stables for **Charles E. Roberts** (Oak Park, Ill.); **Romeo and Juliet Windmill Tower** (near Spring Green, Wis.).

**1897** Houses for **George Furbeck** and **Rollin Furbeck** (both Oak Park, Ill.); boathouse for **Henry Wallis** (Lake Delavan, Wis., demolished).

**1898** River Forest Golf Club (River Forest, Ill., demolished).

**1899** House for **Joseph Husser** (Chicago, Ill., demolished); house remodeled for **Edward C. Waller** (River Forest, Ill., demolished).

What captured Wright's imagination at the '93 fair was Ho-o-Den, the replica of a 1053 Kyoto complex. The structures' substantial rooflines contrasting with lighter—and natural-light-transmitting—bodies, and their low-lying proportions, would trigger a lifelong affinity for **Japanese traditions** already piqued by the interest he had in *hashirakake* prints.

Wright immediately integrated these ideas into his residential work. His interest in "light screens"—notable for their restrained palette and elegant geometries—led to experimentation with prismatic glass tiles (known as Luxfer Prisms).

1900 Writes "A Philosophy of Fine Art" and "What is Architecture?" (both lectures).

1903 A son, Robert Llewelyn, is born.

1904 Death of his father, William Cary Wright.

1905 Makes first trip to Japan and his interest in collecting Japanese prints deepens.

*Pictures, this page, from left to right:* The William E. Martin House; a planter at the Darwin D. Martin residence; a Japanese Ukiyo-e print, like those on which Wright was so keen; and the entrance to the Heurtley House.

*Pictures, opposite page, from left to right:* The living room at the Beachy House; the Avery Coonley House; the Stockman House; glass and concrete details at "Hollyhock House"; and a vintage postcard featuring Tokyo's Imperial Hotel (bottom right).

1909 Leaves his practice and family and travels to Europe with Mamah Borthwick Cheney.

## 1900 1902 1904 1906 1908

1900  Houses for **William Adams** (Chicago, Ill.), **Harley Bradley**, and **Warren Hickox** (both Kankakee, Ill.); summer cottages for **Stephen A. Foster** (Chicago, Ill.), **E.H. Pitkin** (Sapper Island, Desbarats, Ontario, Canada), and **Henry Wallis** (Lake Delavan, Wis.); boathouse for **Fred B. Jones** (Lake Delavan, Wis.); house remodeled and garage for **Warren McArthur** (Chicago, Ill.).

1901  Houses for **E. Arthur Davenport** (River Forest, Ill.), **William Fricke** and **Frank Thomas** (both Oak Park, Ill.), **F.B. Henderson** (Elmhurst, Ill.), and **Fred B. Jones** (Lake Delavan, Wis.); additions to **River Forest Golf Club** (River Forest, Ill., demolished); poultry house, stables, and gates for **Edward C. Waller** (River Forest, Ill., demolished); gatehouse for **Henry Wallis** (Lake Delavan, Wis.); exhibition pavilion for **Universal Portland Cement Company** (Buffalo, N.Y., demolished); **Hillside Home School** (near Spring Green, Wis.).

The first decade of the new century saw Wright developing designs for his **Prairie houses**, which are characterized by long, low lines, shallow-pitched roofs with projecting eaves, and, internally, open spaces filled with natural light, in contrast to the boxlike rooms of the homes of the Victorian era.

1902  Houses for **Susan Lawrence Dana** (Springfield, Ill.), **Arthur Heurtley** and **William E. Martin** (both Oak Park, Ill.), **Francis W. Little** (Peoria, Ill.), **Charles R. Ross** and **George W. Spencer** (both Lake Delavan, Wis.), and **Ward W. Willits** (Highland Park, Ill.); double cottage for **George Gerts** and cottage for **Walter Gerts** (both Whitehall, Mich.); house remodeled for **Arthur Heurtley** (Les Cheneaux Club, Marquette Island, Mich.).

1903  Houses for **George Barton** (Buffalo, N.Y.), **Edwin H. Cheney** (Oak Park, Ill.), and **J.J. Walser** (Chicago, Ill.); barn, stables, and gatehouse for **Fred B. Jones** (Lake Delavan, Wis.); **Abraham Lincoln Center** for Jenkin Lloyd Jones (Chicago, Ill.); **Larkin Company Administration Building** (Buffalo, N.Y., demolished); fountain for **Scoville Park** (Oak Park, Ill.).

Wright's first significant public work was the **Larkin Company Administration Building** (Buffalo, 1903). Seizing the opportunity to apply his open-plan ideas and vision of humanist architecture to the workplace, he created an imposing steel-and-concrete, red-brick-surfaced, stone-trimmed monolith. Inside, vertically stacked tiers overlooked an immense, skylighted central court filled with neatly aligned rows of desks, each surrounded by secretaries.

1904  Houses for **Robert M. Lamp** (Madison, Wis.), **Darwin D. Martin** (Buffalo, N.Y.), and **Burton J. Westcott** (Springfield, Ohio).

1905  Houses for **Mary M.W. Adams** (Highland Park, Ill.), **Charles E. Brown** (Evanston, Ill.), **W.A. Glasner** (Glencoe, Ill.), **Thomas P. Hardy** (Racine, Wis.), **William R. Heath** (Buffalo, N.Y.), and **A.P. Johnson** (Lake Delavan, Wis.); three summer cottages for **Mrs. Thomas Gale** (Whitehall, Mich.); gardener's cottage for **Darwin D. Martin** (Buffalo, N.Y.); real-estate office for **E.A. Cummings** (River Forest, Ill., demolished); **E-Z Polish Factory** for William E. and Darwin Martin (Chicago, Ill.); **Lawrence Memorial Library** (Dana House, Springfield, Ill.); interior remodeled of **Rookery Building** (Chicago, Ill.); bank for **Frank L. Smith** (Dwight, Ill.); **Unity Temple** (Oak Park, Ill.).

Much of Wright's work in the Buffalo area had a connection to the Larkin Building, notably the house (1904) and gardener's cottage (1905) that he created for the company's general manager, **Darwin D. Martin**. Martin would become a lifelong friend and patron; his 10,000-square-foot (929-square-meter) house—a pure expression of the Prairie period, it has arguably unrivaled art-glass installations—is considered one of Wright's best.

1906  Houses for **K.C. DeRhodes** (South Bend, Ind.), **Grace Fuller** (Glencoe, Ill., demolished), **A.W. Gridley** (Batavia, Ill.), **E.R. Hills** (Oak Park, Ill.), **P.D. Hoyt** (Geneva, Ill.), **George Madison Millard** (Highland Park, Ill.), and **Frederick Nicholas** (Flossmoor, Ill.); house remodeled for **P.A. Beachy** (Oak Park, Ill.); **Pettit Mortuary Chapel** (Belvidere, Ill.); **River Forest Tennis Club** (River Forest, Ill.).

1907  Houses for **Avery Coonley** and **F.F. Tomek** (both Riverside, Ill.), **Stephen M.M. Hunt** (La Grange, Ill.), and **Andrew Porter** ("Tan-y-deri," near Spring Green, Wis.); house remodeled for **Col. George Fabyan** (Geneva, Ill.); garage for **George Blossom** (Chicago, Ill.); additions to **Fricke House/Emma Martin House** (Oak Park, Ill.); remodeled **Fox River Country Club** (Geneva, Ill., demolished); **Larkin Company Exhibition Pavilion** (Jamestown, Va., demolished); remodeled **Pebbles and Balch Shop** (Oak Park, Ill., demolished).

Wright's frequent use of **cantilevers**—load-bearing beams that are supported at only one end—gave rise to the defining characteristics of some of his most iconic creations. At the Robie House (among many others), cantilevers enabled him to fill a nonstructural wall with an expanse of art glass.

1908  Houses for **E.E. Boynton** (Rochester, N.Y.), **Walter V. Davidson** (Buffalo, N.Y.), **Robert W. Evans** (Chicago, Ill.), **L.K. Horner** (Chicago, Ill., demolished), **Eugene A. Gilmore** (Madison, Wis.), **Meyer May** (Grand Rapids, Mich.), **Isabel Roberts** (River Forest, Ill.), **Dr. G.C. Stockman** (Mason City, Iowa), and **Frederick C. Robie** (Chicago, Ill.); **Browne's Bookstore** (Chicago, Ill., demolished); garage for **William H. Copeland** (Oak Park, Ill.).

1909  Houses for **J.H. Amberg*** (Grand Rapids, Mich.), **Frank J. Baker** (Wilmette, Ill.), **Hiram Baldwin** (Kenilworth, Ill.), **Mrs. Thomas Gale** (Oak Park, Ill.), **Kibben Ingalls** (River Forest, Ill.), **E.P. Irving** and **Robert Mueller*** (both Decatur, Ill.), **Oscar M. Steffens** (Chicago, Ill., demolished), and **George Stewart** (Montecito, Calif.); **Blythe-Markley City National Bank and Hotel** (Mason City, Iowa); **Como Orchards Summer Colony** (Darby, Mont.); **Bitter Root Inn** (near Darby, Mont., demolished); **Stohr Arcade and Shops** and **Thurber's Art Gallery, Fine Arts Building** (both Chicago, Ill., both demolished); bathing pavilion for **Edward C. Waller** (Charlevoix, Mich.); additions to the **Little House/Robert Clark House** (Peoria, Ill.); house remodeled for **William H. Copeland** (Oak Park, Ill.). *Note: the asterisked houses are also attributed to Marion Mahony, who supervised work when Wright left for Europe.

**1910** Returns from Italy, having arranged for the publication in Europe of a folio detailing his designs (*Ausgeführte Bauten und Entwürfe von Frank Lloyd Wright,* or *Studies and Executed Buildings by Frank Lloyd Wright*), published by Ernst Wasmuth (Berlin, Germany).

**1912** Opens an office in Orchestra Hall, Chicago, Ill. *The Japanese Print: An Interpretation* published.

**1913** Visits Japan.

**1914** Mamah Borthwick Cheney, her two children, and four others are murdered by a servant, who then sets fire to Taliesin I; a month later, Wright starts to rebuild it.

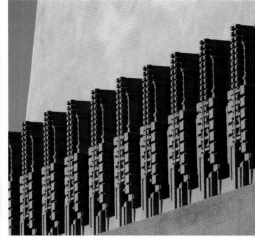

**1916** Travels to Japan with Miriam Noel. Opens an office in Tokyo.

**1918** Travels to China as a guest of the Chinese scholar Ku Hung Ming.

## 1910   1912   1914   1916   1918

**1910** Universal Portland Cement Company Exhibition Pavilion (Madison Square Garden, New York, N.Y., demolished); house for Reverend J.R. Ziegler (Frankfort, Ky.).

**1911** Houses for **Herbert Angster** (Lake Bluff, Ill., demolished) and **O.B. Balch** (Oak Park, Ill.); **Banff Park Pavilion** (Banff National Park, Alberta, Canada, demolished); playhouse, gardener's cottage, and stables for **Avery Coonley** (Riverside, Ill.); **Lake Geneva Inn** (Lake Geneva, Wis., demolished); **Taliesin I** (near Spring Green, Wis., partly demolished).

Having left for Europe with his mistress in 1909, Wright began **the new decade** in Fiesole, near Florence, Italy, from where he visited Berlin, Germany, preparing his Wasmuth portfolio of drawings. Returning to Oak Park the following year, he found his business adversely affected by the scandal of his affair and abandoned wife and family. Yet despite his reduced commissions during the following years, his time in Europe had given him the opportunity to study its art and architecture, inspiring him, along with his subsequent visits to Japan, to try new creative possibilities.

The tragic murder in 1914 of Mamah Cheney affected him profoundly, but Wright set about rebuilding Taliesin, trying to find solace in work.

**1912** Houses for **William B. Greene** (Aurora, Ill.) and **Francis W. Little** (Wayzata, Minn.); remodeling of **Park Ridge Country Club** (Park Ridge, Ill., demolished).

**1913** House for **Harry S. Adams** (Oak Park, Ill.); **Midway Gardens** (Chicago, Ill., demolished); **Imperial Hotel** (Tokyo, Japan, demolished).

July 1914 saw the grand opening of Wright's period extravaganza, **Midway Gardens**. Occupying a full square block on Chicago's South Side, and comprising both winter and summer gardens, it provided a new kind of leisure and dining space for urban dwellers.

In execution Midway Gardens was Wright at his intuitive best. The first large public project for which he designed everything, inside and out (he pronounced it his most complete "work of art"), it was initially hugely popular. Surely drawn by the broad entertainment possibilities, the crowds were responding as well to Wright's vital expression of "pure form"—seen in its strolling gardens and in its many balconies and terraces, all with dance-floor views and enhanced by their artfully embossed cast-concrete construction. Prohibition dampened this sparkling social scene, however; in 1929 the entire complex was bulldozed.

**1914** Taliesin II (near Spring Green, Wis.).

**1915** Houses for **Emil Bach** (Chicago, Ill.), **Sherman Booth**, and **E.D. Brigham** (both Glencoe, Ill.); **Ravine Bluffs Bridge and Housing** (Glencoe, Ill.); **A.D. German Warehouse** (Richland Center, Wis.).

In 1916—three years after he'd begun sketches for it—Wright was awarded a coveted commission for **Tokyo's Imperial Hotel**. Here he demonstrated not only an aesthetic sensitivity to the natural terrain, but understood that the structure must withstand the region's earthquakes. Also influenced by the site's direct proximity to the Imperial Palace, he allowed his respect for historic Japanese forms to supersede a preference for modernity.

Designed to ensure a low center of gravity, a floating foundation supported the elegant reinforced-concrete-and-brick building; the roof was clad with lightweight copper.

Given the criticism he faced after he returned to the USA, Wright was especially rewarded when, in the aftermath of the 1923 Great Kanto Earthquake, he received this telegram from Baron Kihachiro Okura:
*Hotel stands undamaged as monument to your genius. Congratulations.*

**1916** Houses for **Joseph Bagley, W.S. Carr**, and **Ernest Vosburgh** (all Grand Beach, Mich.), **Frederick C. Bogk** and **Arthur L. Richard** (two) (all in Milwaukee, Wis.); American System Ready-cut duplex apartments for **Arthur Munkwitz** (Milwaukee, Wis., demolished) and **Richards Company** (Milwaukee, Wis.).

**1917** Houses for **Henry J. Allen** (Wichita, Kans.), **Aline Barnsdall** ("Hollyhock House," Los Angeles, Calif.), **Aisaku Hayashi** (Tokyo, Japan), and **Stephen M.B. Hunt** (Oshkosh, Wis.).

Wright's Japanese **assistants** for the Imperial Hotel, like Marion Mahony in his Oak Park years, were fine artisans in their own right. The machine techniques that Wright usually revered—and that were used so effectively for Mahony's exquisite stained glasswork and mosaics—were supplanted in Tokyo by handcrafted ornamentation from local oya stone.

**1918** Houses for **Arinobu Fukuhara** (Hakone, Japan, demolished) and **Tazaemon Yamamura** (Ashiya, Japan).

Details of Midway Gardens and the Imperial Hotel anticipated Wright's **Mayan-influenced** Californian residences. Emulating historic works of the Yucatán, such as Palenque, these 1920s' structures employed staggered massing, vertical stelelike elements, and extensive use of deep-relief, cast-concrete forms.

Wright credited his grounding in geometry to his childhood Froebel toys. He employed a **modular system of design**, in which plans were built upon repeating units of a particular shape—squares, rectangles, parallelograms, and hexagons being favorites, the latter two leading to interesting angles and forms in the interior spaces. In a number of his Usonian homes, including the William Palmer and Roland Reisley houses, the grid is scored directly into the concrete floor.

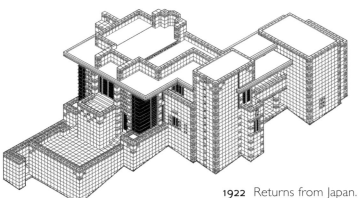

**1922** Returns from Japan. Is divorced from Catherine.

**1923** Opens an office in Los Angeles, Calif. Death of his mother, Anna Lloyd Jones Wright. *Experimenting with Human Lives* published. Marries Miriam Noel.

**1924** Miriam Noel leaves. Wright meets Olga (Olgivanna) Lazovich.

**1925** A second major fire breaks out at Taliesin; Wright rebuilds it as Taliesin III. A daughter, Iovanna, is born to him and Olgivanna.

**1926** The Bank of Wisconsin appropriates Taliesin's title due to Wright's indebtedness. Wright is arrested near Minneapolis, Minn., for being in violation of the Mann Act. Starts writing his autobiography.

**1927** Begins to write monthly articles for the *Architectural Record*, which are published under the heading "In the Cause of Architecture." Is divorced from Miriam Noel. Visits Puerto Rico with Olgivanna, and the couple spend the winter in Phoenix, Ariz.

**1928** Marries Olgivanna at Rancho Santa Fe, Calif. Wright, Inc., is established by friends, who obtain the title to Taliesin on his behalf.

## 1920 · 1922 · 1924 · 1926 · 1928

**1920** "Residence A" and "Residence B" (demolished) for **Aline Barnsdall** (Olive Hill, Los Angeles, Calif.).

**1921** Jiyu Gakuen School (Tokyo, Japan).

Wright spent almost four years in Japan, with Noel, supervising construction of the Imperial Hotel. Immersing himself in the culture, he adopted a Japanese lifestyle, studied the architecture, and expanded his already extensive collection of Japanese prints. In addition to three houses in Tokyo, he designed the alternative Jiyu Gakuen School ("Freedom School") for girls there; its aim was to produce independent, creative thinkers. He continued work on Hollyhock House during his stay in Japan.

Returning to the USA in 1922, Wright developed his Californian designs, using new techniques in concrete construction. His relationship with Noel soured, however, and the following years saw Wright plagued by his **turbulent personal life**, compounded by legal problems and debt, which led to the temporary loss of his home, Taliesin. But he found a true soulmate when he met Olgivanna Lazovich, whom he married in 1928, bringing much-needed stability to his life and creating the conditions for a happier, more productive and creative time of life.

**1922** Interior design, own studio at rented property at **Harper Avenue** (Los Angeles, Calif.).

**1923** Houses for **John Storer** (Los Angeles, Calif.) and **Alice Millard** ("La Miniatura," Pasadena, Calif.); house rebuilt for **Nathan G. Moore** (Oak Park, Ill.).

Wright's **textile-block construction system** uses blocks of concrete, usually cast on site and molded with a decorative motif, sometimes pierced to allow light through, and reinforced with steel. The blocks were grooved at the edges so that they could be stacked with steel rods in between. Concrete was then poured in to reinforce and grout.

**1924** Houses for **Charles Ennis** and **Samuel Freeman** (Los Angeles, Calif.).

**1925** **Taliesin III** (near Spring Green, Wis.).

Wright's work became more abstract, and more explicitly geometric, as his career progressed. His circles, spirals, and cubes sprang not only from the **Froebel "gifts"** of childhood, but from their symbolic, "essential" meanings, the circle, for example, representing unity, the square, integrity, and the triangle, aspiration. The Froebel training also included exercises in drawing on grid-lined paper and weaving with strips of paper; Wright referred to his 1920s work in concrete blocks as "weaving."

**1927** **Arizona Biltmore Hotel** and cottages (Phoenix, Ariz.; *Wright acted as consultant and was not credited as architect of record*); house for **Darwin D. Martin** ("Graycliff House," Derby, N.Y.); **Ras-el-Bar**, beach cottages (Damyat, Egypt, demolished).

Controversy over authorship of the **Arizona Biltmore Hotel** remains a factor in assessing this period in Wright's work. Ostensibly retained as a consultant for the fabrication and design of the building's distinctive textile-block façade, Wright's imprint is apparent throughout. While official credit goes to Albert Chase McArthur, a former Wright apprentice and the project's codeveloper, documents relating to the 1927 design indicate that Wright may have had legal reasons to avoid sharing the limelight.

**1928** Own desert compound and studio ("Ocatilla," near Chandler, Ariz., demolished).

**1929** Camp cabins for the **Chandler Land Improvement Co.** (Chandler, Ariz., demolished); house for **Richard Lloyd Jones** (Tulsa, Okla.).

**The late 1920s** were fraught not only personally, but professionally, for Wright. No sooner had he gotten reinstated at Taliesin—thanks to Philip La Follette, Wright's intrepid lawyer—and begun to assess its woeful condition, when he was approached for another Arizona project. The ambitious San Marcos-in-the-Desert resort plan would inspire him greatly, but the 1929 financial crash ensured that it, and other recent commissions (including a New York apartment tower, St. Mark's-in-the-Bouwerie), would never get built.

The news in 1929 that Midway Gardens had succumbed to the wrecking ball was another dismal coda to what Wright called his "nightmare decade."

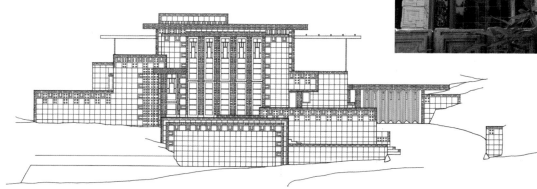

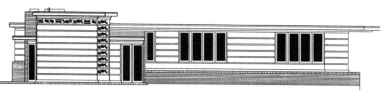

*Opposite, top, from left to right:*
*Aerial isometric of the Freeman House, with block details from that and the Storer House (below); the Ennis House's south façade; and a portrait of Wright in 1926.*

**1931** Visits Rio de Janeiro, Brazil. *Modern Architecture*, a collection of lectures delivered in 1930, and *The Hillside Home School of the Allied Arts: Why We Want This School*, published.

*This page, top, from left to right:*
*East elevation of the Loren Pope House; reception hall of the Johnson Wax Building; and details at the Anne Pfeiffer Chapel and Loren Pope House.*

**1932** Wright and Olgivanna found the Taliesin Fellowship. *An Autobiography* and *The Disappearing City* published.

**1934** The first issue of *Taliesin* (a magazine) is published by the Taliesin Press.

**1937** Wright and Olgivanna travel to Russia. *Architecture and Modern Life* is published in collaboration with Baker Brownell. Buys a large section of government land near Phoenix, Ariz., on which to construct Taliesin West. The Taliesin Fellowship initiates its annual custom of migrating between Wisconsin and Arizona.

**1938** Appears on the cover of *Time* magazine.

**1939** Travels to London, England, to deliver a series of lectures, which is published as *An Organic Architecture*.

## 1930  1932  1934  1936  1938

Wright was in his sixties during **the Depression years**, with an extraordinary career behind him. Rather than quitting while there were few commissions to be found, however, he wrote and lectured extensively, publishing the first edition of his autobiography in 1932, which revealed both the philosophy behind his designs and his passion for his life's work. Many critics believed that Wright's work had been eclipsed by the International Style, which Wright decried as soulless. On the contrary, his "organic architecture" began to find full expression at what seemed his most fallow point. Founding the Taliesin Fellowship in 1932, he went on to design the iconic Fallingwater and other masterpieces, including the technically virtuosic Johnson Wax complex and his desert home and compound, Taliesin West.

When Wright founded the **Taliesin Fellowship**, he created a new foundation for his practice and secured his legacy. The Fellowship was an apprenticeship system, with full room and board provided. The work at hand was as much about repairing Taliesin as learning the trade, and immersion in the soul of Wright's enterprise.

The dedicated troop—Edgar Tafel, Wesley Peters, and Jack Howe were among the first to sign on—came along in 1937, when Wright decamped to Taliesin West, seeking a warmer place in which to winter. Begun with simple redwood framing and canvas covers—similar to his camp "Ocatilla"—Taliesin West became a laboratory for all that would follow.

As Wright viewed it, the modern city was a scourge, a "parasite of the spirit." His 1932 publication *The Disappearing City* posited a new model for a troubled America—a community that would bring people closer to their environment. The 12-foot-square (1.1-meter-square) model of his utopian vision, **Broadacre City**, presented such a plan.

**1932** Taliesin Fellowship Complex (near Spring Green, Wis.).

**1933** Hillside Playhouse (near Spring Green, Wis.).

**1934** House for **Malcolm Willey** (Minneapolis, Minn.); construction of scale model of a section of **Broadacre City** begun.

**1935** Completed **Broadacre City** model exhibited at National Alliance of Arts and Industry Exposition (Rockefeller Center, New York, N.Y.); houses for **Edgar J. Kaufmann, Sr.** ("Fallingwater," Bear Run, Pa.) and **Paul R.** and **Jean Hanna** ("Honeycomb House," Stanford, Calif.).

**1936** Houses for **Herbert Jacobs** (Madison, Wis.) and **Mrs. Abby Beecher Roberts** ("Deertrack House," Marquette, Mich.); **S.C. Johnson & Son Co. Administration Building** (Johnson Wax) (Racine, Wis.).

**1937** Houses for **Herbert F. Johnson** ("Wingspread House," Racine, Wis.) and **Ben Rebhuhn** (Great Neck Estates, N.Y.); **Taliesin West** (Scottsdale, Ariz.); office for **Edgar J. Kaufmann, Sr.** (Pittsburgh, Pa., dismantled, though later reinstalled at the Victoria & Albert Museum, London, UK).

**1938** First design submitted for **Olin Terraces** (Madison, Wis.); **Florida Southern College Master Plan** for Dr. Ludd M. Spivey (Lakeland, Fla.); **Anne Pfeiffer Chapel, Florida Southern College** (Lakeland, Fla.); houses for **Ralph Jester** (Palos Verdes, Calif., later executed for **Arthur** and **Bruce Brooks Pfeiffer**, Scottsdale, Ariz.) and **Charles Manson** (Wausau, Wis.); guest house for **Edgar J. Kaufmann, Sr.** (Bear Run, Pa.); **Midway Barns** and farm buildings, **Taliesin** (near Spring Green, Wis.); **Sun Top Homes** for Otto Mallery and the Todd Company (Ardmore, Pa.); **Auldbrass House and Plantation** buildings for Leigh Stevens (Yemassee, S.C.).

**1939** Houses for **L.N. Bell** (Los Angeles, Calif., later executed for **Joe Feldmann**, Berkeley, Calif.), **Andrew F.H. Armstrong** (Ogden Dunes, Ind.), **Sidney Bazett** (Hillsborough, Calif.), **Joseph Euchtman** (Baltimore, Md.), **Lloyd Lewis** (Libertyville, Ill.), **Rose** and **Gertrude Pauson** (Phoenix, Ariz.), **John C. Pew** (Madison, Wis.), **Loren Pope** (Falls Church, Va.), **Stanley Rosenbaum** (Florence, Ala.), **Bernard Schwartz** (Two Rivers, Wis.), **George Sturges** (Brentwood Heights, Los Angeles, Calif.), and **Kathrine Winckler** and **Alma Goetsch** (Okemos, Mich.).

*Pictures, opposite page, from left to right:* An art-glass window and concrete blocks at the Ennis House; a diagram of the south elevation of the John Storer residence; and the Arizona Biltmore Hotel.

*This page, from left to right:* Fallingwater's guest house viewed from the main house; Fallingwater viewed on approach from the driveway; the George Sturges House; and interior details at the Anne Pfeiffer Chapel.

**1940** A major retrospective exhibition, entitled by Wright "The Work of Frank Lloyd Wright: In the Nature of Materials," is mounted at the Museum of Modern Art, New York, N.Y. The museum chooses to call it "Frank Lloyd Wright, American Architect," and the show runs with both titles. Establishes the Frank Lloyd Wright Foundation.

**1941** Publishes *On Architecture* (with Frederick Gutheim). The Taliesin Press publishes a second issue of *Taliesin* and five issues of *A Taliesin Square-Paper: A Nonpolitical Voice from Our Democratic Minority*.

*This page: The 1948 houses for Mrs. Clinton Walker (right) and Curtis Meyer (far right); and, pictured below, the 1944 S.C. Johnson & Son Co. Research Tower (left) and the 1946 Unitarian Meeting House (right).*

*Opposite page, from left to right: Details and façade of the 1954 Hagan House; Wright, photographed in the same year; the 1955 Turkel House; the 1959 Lykes House; and, pictured below, Roland Reisley's 1951 house in the community of Usonia (left) and the 1959 Grady Gammage Memorial Auditorium (right).*

**1943** A revised edition of *An Autobiography* and *Book Six: Broadacre City* are published.

**1944** An issue of *A Taliesin Square-Paper* is published.

**1945** *When Democracy Builds* is published, as well as two issues of *A Taliesin Square-Paper*.

**1946** Svetlana, Wright's stepdaughter, is killed in an automobile accident. An issue of *A Taliesin Square-Paper* is published.

**1948** Taliesin Press publishes a brochure, *Taliesin to Friends*.

**1949** Publishes *Genius and the Mobocracy*.

## 1940 · 1942 · 1944 · 1946 · 1948

**1940** Houses for **Gregor Affleck** (Bloomfield Hills, Mich.), **Theodore Baird** (Amherst, Mass.), **James Christie** (Bernardsville, N.J.), and **Clarence Sondern** (Kansas City, Mo.); **Community Church** (Kansas City, Mo.); **Seminar Buildings, Florida Southern College** (Lakeland, Fla.); gatehouse for **Arch Oboler** (Malibu, Calif.).

**1941** Roux Library, Florida Southern College (Lakeland, Fla.); houses for **Roy Peterson** (Racine, Wis., later executed for Haddock, Ann Arbor, Mich.), **Stuart Richardson** (Glen Ridge, N.J.), and **Carlton D. Wall** ("**Snowflake House**," Detroit, Mich.); retreat for **Arch Obolor** (Malibu, Calif.).

A criticism widely leveled at Wright, and not without some justification, was his profligacy, as he frequently blew his construction budgets in spectacular style, as well as craving the finer things in life and failing to keep track of his personal debts. Far from being an architect focused solely on lavish, high-profile projects, though, he considered his **Usonian homes**, developed for those on a modest budget, among his most important achievements. These beautiful, functional, smaller residences, which became sought-after in the 1940s, defined new standards for domestic architecture. Their interiors still look fresh today.

**1942** Industrial Arts Building, Florida Southern College (Lakeland, Fla.).

**1943** Original design for **Solomon R. Guggenheim Museum** (New York, N.Y.); farm unit for **Lloyd Lewis** (Libertyville, Ill.); Solar Hemicycle House for **Herbert Jacobs** (Middleton, Wis.).

In the 1943 **Herbert Jacobs House**, Wright built on earlier ideas to create a precursor of today's energy-conscious homes. The "solar hemicycle" house was designed to conserve warmth in the winter, by being partially built into the earth and oriented to make the most of winter sun, and to stay cool in summer because its overhanging roof shades the house from overhead sunlight.

**1944** S.C. Johnson & Son Co. (Johnson Wax) Research Tower (Racine, Wis.).

**1945** Administration Building, Florida Southern College (Lakeland, Fla.); lodge for **Arnold Friedman** (Pecos, N.M.); house for **Lowell Walter** (Cedar Rock, Quasqueton, Iowa); **Taliesin Dams** (near Spring Green, Wis.).

In the 1940s Wright produced several schemes for alternative communities, believing that the built environment could be designed to enhance quality of life. One such was **Usonia**, a cooperative utopian community near Pleasantville, New York, incorporated by a group of idealistic young couples in 1945. Wright designed the site plan for 47 residences and houses for Sol Friedman, Edward Serlin, and Roland Reisley, who said in a 2008 interview: "There has not been a day of my life when I did not see something beautiful in this house."

**1946** Houses for **Amy Alpaugh** (Northport, Mich.), **Douglas Grant** (Cedar Rapids, Iowa), **Chauncey Griggs** (Tacoma, Wash.), **Dr. Alvin Miller** (Charles City, Iowa), and **Melvyn Maxwell Smith** (Bloomfield Hills, Mich.); **Esplanades, Florida Southern College** (Lakeland, Fla.); **Unitarian Meeting House** (Shorewood Hills, Wis.).

**1947** House for **Dr. A.H. Bulbulian** (Rochester, Minn.); dairy and machine shed, **Midway Barns, Taliesin** (near Spring Green, Wis.); **Parkwyn Village Housing Master Plan** (Kalamazoo, Mich.); **Usonia II Housing Master Plan** (Pleasantville, N.Y.).

Wright designed a number of **houses of worship** for various faith communities during the course of his career, most of which were built during his later years. The son of a minister, and with a deep sense of the spiritual, he displayed a profound understanding of sacred concepts, creating innovative and memorable spaces for contemplation and prayer. Religious symbols were incorporated into the form of these structures, as, for example, at the Beth Sholom Synagogue, which bears a stylized menorah on each of its structural beams, and the Annunciation Greek Orthodox Church, whose design is based on the Greek cross.

**1948** Houses for **Albert Adelman** (Fox Point, Wis.), **Carroll Alsop** and **Jack Lamberson** (both Oskaloosa, Iowa), **Erling Brauner** (Okemos, Mich.), **Maynard Buehler** (Orinda, Calif.), **Samuel Eppstein**, **Curtis Meyer**, **Eric Pratt**, and **David Weisblat** (all Galesburg, Mich.), **Sol Friedman** (Usonia II, Pleasantville, N.Y.), **Willis Hughes** (Jackson, Miss.), **Herman T. Mossberg** (South Bend, Ind.), **Robert Levin** (Kalamazoo, Mich.), **Charles T. Weltzheimer** (Oberlin, Ohio), and **Mrs. Clinton Walker** (Carmel, Calif.); **Sun Cottage** for **Iovanna Lloyd Wright** (Taliesin West, Scottsdale, Ariz.); additions to the **Sondern House** for **Arnold Adler** (Kansas City, Mo.), to the guest house for **Edgar J. Kaufmann, Sr.** (Bear Run, Pa.), and to the house for **Stanley Rosenbaum** (Florence, Ala.); **Water Dome, Florida Southern College** (Lakeland, Fla.); gift shop for **V.C. Morris** (San Francisco, Calif.); boathouse and river pavilion for **Lowell Walter** (Quasqueton, Iowa).

**1949** Houses for **Howard Anthony** (Benton Harbor, Mich.), **Eric Brown** and **Ward McCartney** (Kalamazoo, Mich.), **James Edwards** (Okemos, Mich.), **Kenneth Laurent** (Rockford, Ill.), **Henry J. Neils** (Minneapolis, Minn.), and **Edward Serlin** (Usonia II, Pleasantville, N.Y.); **Cabaret Theater, Taliesin West** (Scottsdale, Ariz.).

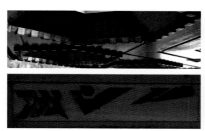

**1951** With the architect's cooperation, Oscar Stonorov creates a traveling exhibition of Wright's work entitled "Sixty Years of Living Architecture," which opens at the Palazzo Strozzi in Florence, Italy. Wright opens a West Coast office in San Francisco with an associate, Aaron Green.

**1952** The Hillside Home School buildings in Spring Green, Wis., are partially destroyed by fire.

**1953** Publishes *The Future of Architecture*.

**1954** Publishes *The Natural House*.

**1955** Publishes *An American Architecture*, in collaboration with Edgar Kaufmann, Jr. Establishes "Taliesin East," an office and residence at the Plaza Hotel, New York, N.Y.

**1956** Publishes *The Story of the Tower*.

**1957** Travels to Baghdad, Iraq; London, England; Paris, France; and Cairo, Egypt. Publishes *A Testament*.

**1959** Begins writing *The Wonderful World of Architecture*, which remains unpublished. Dies on April 9 in Arizona.

## 1950 · 1952 · 1954 · 1956 · 1958

**1950** Houses for **Robert Berger** (San Anselmo, Calif.), **Raymond Carlson** (Phoenix, Ariz.), **John O. Carr** (Glenview, Ill.), **Dr. Richard Davis** (Marion, Ind.), **S.P. Elam** (Austin, Minn.), **John A. Gillin** (Dallas, Tex.), **Dr. Ina Harper** (St. Joseph, Mich.), **John Haynes** (Fort Wayne, Ind.), **Thomas E. Keys** (Rochester, Minn.), **Arthur Mathews** (Atherton, Calif.), **Robert Muirhead** (Plato Center, Ill.), **William Palmer** (Ann Arbor, Mich.), **Wilbur Pearce** (Bradbury, Calif.), **Don Schaberg** (Okemos, Mich.), **Seymour Shavin** (Chattanooga, Tenn.), **Richard Smith** (Jefferson, Wis.), **Karl A. Staley** (North Madison, Ohio), **J.A. Sweeton** (Cherry Hill, N.J.), **Robert Winn** (Kalamazoo, Mich.), **David Wright** (Phoenix, Ariz.), and **Isadore J. Zimmerman** (Manchester, N.H.); **Southwest Christian Seminary** for **Peyton Canary** (Glendale, Ariz., later executed for the **First Christian Church**, Phoenix, Ariz.).

**1951** Houses for **Benjamin Adelman** (Phoenix, Ariz.), **Gabrielle Austin** (Greenville, S.C.), **W.L. Fuller** (Pass Christian, Miss., demolished), **Charles F. Glore** (Lake Forest, Ill.), **Patrick Kinney** (Lancaster, Wis.), **Russell Kraus** (Kirkwood, Mo.), **Roland Reisley** (Usonia II, Pleasantville, N.Y.), and **Dr. Nathan Rubin** (Canton, Ohio); summer cottage for **A.K. Chahroudi** (Lake Mahopac, N.Y.); **Wetmore Auto Service Station** remodeled (Ferndale, Mich.).

**1952** Houses for **Quentin Blair** (Cody, Wyo.), **Ray Brandes** (Issaquah, Wash.), **George Lewis** (Tallahassee, Fla.), **R.W. Lindholm** (Cloquet, Minn.), **Luis Marden** (McLean, Va.), **Arthur Pieper** (Paradise Valley, Ariz.), and **Frank Sander** (Stamford, Conn.); **Anderton Court Shops** (Beverly Hills, Calif.); **Hillside Theater** (near Spring Green, Wis.); **Price Tower** for the H.C. Price Company (Bartlesville, Okla.); studio-residence for **Archie Teater** (Bliss, Idaho).

**1953** Houses for **Andrew B. Cooke** (Virginia Beach, Va.), **John Dobkins** (Canton, Ohio), **Robert Llewellyn Wright** (Bethesda, Md.), **Lewis Goddard** (Plymouth, Mich.), **Louis Penfield** (Willoughby Hills, Ohio), and **Harold Price, Jr.** (Bartlesville, Okla.); cottage for **Jorgine Boomer** (Phoenix, Ariz.); **Science and Cosmography Building, Florida Southern College** (Lakeland, Fla.); **Beth Sholom Synagogue** (Elkins Park, Pa.); **Taliesin West Sign**, Taliesin (Scottsdale, Ariz.); **Riverview Terrace Restaurant** (Spring Green, Wis.); **Usonian exhibition house and pavilion** for "Sixty Years of Living Architecture" (New York, N.Y., dismantled).

**1954** Houses for **E. Clarke Arnold** (Columbus, Wis.), **Bachman and Wilson** (Millstone, N.J.), **Cedric Boulter** (Cincinnati, Ohio), **John E. Christian** (West Lafayette, Ind.), **Ellis Feiman** (Canton, Ohio), **Louis B. Frederick** (Barrington Hill, Ill.), **Dr. Maurice Greenberg** (Dousman, Wis.), **I.N. Hagan** (Chalkhill, Pa.), **Willard Keland** (Racine, Wis.), **William Thaxton** (Houston, Tex.), and **Gerald Tonkens** (Cincinnati, Ohio); grandma house for **Harold Price, Jr.** (Paradise Valley, Ariz.); guest house for **David Wright** (Phoenix, Ariz.); **Danforth Chapel, Florida Southern College** (Lakeland, Fla.); auto showroom for **Max Hoffman** (New York, N.Y.); **exhibition pavilion** for "Sixty Years of Living Architecture" (Los Angeles, Calif.); own apartment remodeled at **Plaza Hotel** (New York, N.Y.).

**1955** Houses for **Randall Fawcett** (Los Banos, Calif.), **Max Hoffman** (Rye, N.Y.), **Dr. Toufic Kalil** (Manchester, N.H.), **Don Lovness** (Stillwater, Minn.), **T.A. Pappas** (St. Louis, Mo.), **John Rayward** (New Canaan, Conn.), **Robert H. Sunday** (Marshaltown, Iowa), **W.B. Tracy** (Normandy Park, Wash.), and **Dr. Dorothy Turkel** (Detroit, Mich.); **Annunciation Greek Orthodox Church** (Wauwatosa, Wis.); **Dallas Theater Center** for Paul Baker (Dallas, Tex.); **Kundert Medical Clinic** (San Luis Obispo, Calif.).

**1956** Houses for **Frank Bott** (Kansas City, Mo.), **Allen Friedman** (Bannockburn, Ill.), **Frank Iber** (Stevens Point, Wis.), **Arnold Jackson** (Beaver Dam, Wis.), **Joseph Mollica** (Bayside, Wis.), **Carl Post** (Barrington, Ill.), **Dudley Spencer** (Brandywine Head, Del.), **Dr. Paul Trier** (Des Moines, Iowa), and **Eugene Van Tamelen** (Madison, Wis.); final revised scheme for **Solomon R. Guggenheim Museum** (New York, N.Y.); **Lindholm Service Station** (Cloquet, Minn.); clinic for **Dr. Kenneth Meyers** (Dayton, Ohio); **music pavilion, Taliesin West** (Scottsdale, Ariz.); **Wyoming Valley School** (Wyoming Valley, Wis.).

**1957** Houses for **William Boswell** (Cincinnati, Ohio), **C.E. Gordon** (Aurora, Ore.), **Sterling Kinney** (Amarillo, Tex.), **James B. McBean** (Rochester, Minn.), **Walter Rudin** (Madison, Wis.), **Carl Schultz** (St. Joseph, Mich.), **Dr. Robert Walton** (Modesto, Calif.), and **Duey Wright** (Wausau, Wis.); clinic for **Herman Fasbender** (Hastings, Minn.); **Juvenile Cultural Study Center** (University of Wichita, Kans.); **Marin County Civic Center and Post Office** (San Rafael, Calif.); **Rayward Playhouse** for Victoria and Jennifer Rayward (New Canaan, Conn.).

**1958** Houses for **Dr. George Ablin** (Bakersfield, Calif.), **Paul Olfelt** (St. Louis Park, Minn.), and **Don Stromquist** (Bountiful, Utah); additions to house for **John Rayward** (New Canaan, Conn.); cottages for **Donald** and **Virginia Lovness** (Stillwater, Minn.) and **Seth C. Peterson** (Lake Delton, Wis.); **Lockridge Medical Clinic** (Whitefish, Mont.); **Pilgrim Congregational Church** (Redding, Calif.).

**1959** **Grady Gammage Memorial Auditorium**, Arizona State University (Tempe, Ariz.); House for **Norman Lykes** (Phoenix, Ariz.).

Taliesin West came to epitomize Wrightian **organic architecture**. Built from the sand and stone that the surrounding desert and mesa talus gave up, the site wholly inspired Wright and his team. By the time he died, in 1959, the some twenty winters that he spent here would have hundreds of spectacular residences, the Price Tower, the Guggenheim Museum (completed after he died), and even a plan for a mile-high (1.6-kilometer-high) skyscraper to show for them.

Architecture was forever changed by Wright's extraordinary vision. The Frank Lloyd Wright Foundation at Taliesin West continues his work and protects his remarkable legacy for the future.

# "INEFFABLE HARMONIES"

◨ ◨ ◨

# Beginnings

◨ ◨ ◨

"Proceeding … step by step from generals to particulars, plasticity as a large means in architecture began to grip me and to work its own will. … The old architecture, so far as its grammar went, for me began, literally, to disappear. As if by magic new architectural effects came to life—effects genuinely new in the whole cycle of architecture owing simply to the working of this spiritual principle. Vistas of inevitable simplicity and ineffable harmonies would open, so beautiful to me that I was not only delighted, but often startled. Yes, sometimes amazed."

—*An Autobiography*

*The light filtered through the curved band of filigreed windows, and the drop in ceiling height from the main volume of the dining room—creating a "room within a room"—make this a place of simplicity, harmony, and quiet repose, in the William H. Winslow House (1893–94), River Forest, Illinois (left).*

# BREAKING THE BOX

Frank Lloyd Wright, born in 1867, is regarded by many as the twentieth century's greatest architect, yet although he lived to the age of ninety-one, his ideas and beliefs were formed at the end of the nineteenth century. In *An Autobiography*, Wright wrote with characteristic directness: "Early in life, I had to choose between honest arrogance and hypocritical humility. I chose the former and have seen no occasion to change." This boundless self-confidence, together with Wright's lifelong desire to seek harmony with nature in his work, is characteristic of such key influences throughout his long life as the writers Ralph Waldo Emerson (1803–82) and Henry David Thoreau (1817–62).

In 1908 Wright, who was then forty and had achieved some recognition, chiefly for his ground-breaking Larkin Company Administration Building (1903, demolished 1950) in Buffalo, New York, published a seminal essay, "In the Cause of Architecture," in the *Architectural Record*. Here, in an architectural philosophy that can be seen at work for the rest of his long working life, Wright rethought the spaces that he deemed integral to a building and recommended eliminating unnecessary separate rooms, as well as superfluous ornamentation and detail. His concern to "break the box" of the conventional room plan and achieve spatial continuity by treating wall surfaces simply, and in as unbroken a manner as was feasible, led to a radical reworking of the domestic space, with doors and other openings as part of an integrated structure, with all necessary fittings, and, indeed, as much furniture as was practicable, to be built in. In his constant search for the qualities of harmony and repose that he prized above all others in a domestic interior, Wright himself designed the freestanding furniture and glass for the houses. Each was given its own site-specific motifs and character to achieve a unified, organic whole. Central to his design philosophy was what he termed "a good plan," which is "… the beginning and the end because every good plan is organic … there is more beauty in a fine ground plan than in almost any of its ultimate consequences. In itself it will have the rhythms, masses and proportions of a good decoration if it is the organic plan for an organic building with individual style consistent with materials."

Wright's attempts to create spatial continuity by endeavoring to open up the flow of spaces in internal areas, and to dissolve the boundaries, where appropriate, between the building and its surrounding context, can be seen in his earliest domestic buildings, such as the George Blossom House (1892, Chicago, Illinois) and particularly in his own house and studio at

The house in Oak Park that Wright designed in 1893 for Walter Gale (left) was one of the young architect's earliest residential projects. Its Queen Anne style was fashionable at the time, but nascent signs of distinctively Wrightian ideas may be seen already taking shape here, especially in the overhanging, flared eave at the front, right corner, and the high band of windows encircling the turret.

Designed in 1896, although not built until two years later, the nearby George Smith House (right) also has flared eaves; other features Wright explored here include the prominent chimneys, offset entrance with compact porch, and banded trim, in this case, shingle.

In *An Autobiography*, Wright related how prospective client Nathan Moore approached him in 1895 with pictures of English half-timbered houses and asked for a house "something like this," adding that he did not want to attract ridicule for an unconventional-looking home, like Wright's previous client, William Winslow. The young architect's self-confessed regret at conforming to Moore's request for a Tudor-style house (below and below, left; after 1923 remodeling above first-story level) set him all the more firmly on course to abandon derivative design and reimagine domestic living space in his own way.

Oak Park, the center of his creative activity. He wanted to achieve in practice what he described in words as "vista without, vista within," a characteristic that becomes clear to the visitor through experiencing the extraordinary spaces that he designed throughout his career—from his studio in Oak Park to the Solomon R. Guggenheim Museum (1943–59), New York, New York.

Following a stint working for Joseph Lyman Silsbee, Wright's apprenticeship years (1888–93) with the leading Chicago architectural firm of Adler and Sullivan were a lifelong influence. But Wright was soon to move beyond his mentor, Louis Sullivan, particularly in his integral ornamentation in building designs, and in his development of "a good plan." At the time Chicago was in the midst of an unprecedented building boom, following the fire of 1871 that almost entirely destroyed its downtown area. Louis Sullivan became Wright's *lieber Meister*, German for "beloved master," and his philosophy of architecture was to remain with—and be renewed and enhanced by— his erstwhile pupil, so that Wright would develop Sullivan's famous dictum "form follows function" to the conclusion that "form and function are one." In 1889 Sullivan was also to provide crucial financial support for his young apprentice in the form of a loan of $5000. This enabled the twenty-two-year-old architect to begin building a house (and later practice) for his wife and growing family at Oak Park.

During the years of Wright's apprenticeship, Sullivan and his partner, Dankmar Adler, were commissioned to build major public buildings in what was fast becoming a showcase city. The most famous of these, the Chicago Stock Exchange and the vast and technologically advanced Auditorium Building, were bold in both design and conception. The centerpiece of the thirteen-story, metal-framed Chicago Stock Exchange, the two-story trading room, has been reconstructed in the Art Institute of Chicago, where it provides an invaluable resource for an understanding of Sullivan's "form follows function" idea and its influence on the work of his most famous follower. The vibrant, naturalistic color scheme of the room, with its repeated organic designs in no less than fifty-seven different colors, is enhanced by the natural light from art-glass skylights whose design repeats the suggestion of a verdant space in the middle of the bustling new city. This was a direct precursor of Wright's idea of an inward-looking space, or "vista within," removed from exterior circumstance.

One of Wright's most influential objectives, that of an "organic architecture," also grew from his experience of working on public buildings with the Adler and Sullivan practice. The practice was so busy with major public commissions that domestic work was in the main entrusted to their chief draftsman, as Wright was soon to become, while the partners retained responsibility for the overall supervision of more important commissions.

Wright was always mindful not only of external appearances and layout, but also of interior design, considering the furnishings, fittings, and any decorative objects to be essential elements of a harmonious whole. In the staircase just inside the entrance to his Oak Park house (above), the woodwork, cornicing, and friezes wrap smoothly around corners and angles; wall and floor surfaces are unadorned, finished naturally, and in restful colors. He admired Classical figures and often placed statues like this one in his—and his clients'—homes. The shingled gable dominates the western, Forest Avenue frontage (opposite), the entrance to Wright's house; note the off-center doorway. From this aspect, the original home is reminiscent of the fashionable 1880s' Shingle-style houses built by architects McKim, Mead, and White in Newport, Rhode Island, and other New England resorts.

# "TRUTH IS LIFE"

In 1889 Wright married Catherine Tobin and then, with the loan from his mentor, Louis Sullivan, began building a house in the leafy Chicago suburb of Oak Park. The young architect was able to put his architectural theories into practice over the next twenty years in his adaptations and additions to what started out originally as a modest home. A playroom was added in 1895, and a sizable studio, containing a drafting room, an office, and a library, was added to the house in 1898, a year after Wright moved his office from downtown Chicago to Oak Park. The complex became a dual-purpose space: home and workplace.

Both house and studio were used to experiment with ideas and their implementation, and Wright's imaginative models for refashioned space and form were subject to the practicalities of day-to-day family and working life. It is clear that Wright used the house and studio as a laboratory before applying the lessons learned there to his commissioned work for clients.

The visitor approaching Wright's home and studio today is drawn to the striking and dramatic frontage on Chicago Avenue. Impressive and intricate in its detail, the whole frontage was a grand presence in the progressive and burgeoning suburb of Oak Park. The modest entrance to the original house, with its sheltering, shingle, pyramidal central gable, is on Forest Avenue. The studio, while connected internally, has an entirely separate entrance. Original in design, the ensemble is built of essentially simple and organic materials: brick with stone dressings and dark-wood shingles. The centerpiece of the stepped frontage, which includes the drafting room, library, and Wright's studio, is an entrance loggia with plaster bas-reliefs, designed by Wright and sculpted by Richard Bock, who was to provide ornamental detail for many later projects, including the elaborate sculptural program of the Susan Lawrence Dana House (1902–4). For the exterior elevation of Oak Park, Bock provided the freestanding crouching-figure sculptures, as well as the bas-reliefs of the colonnade that featured storks, which suggest wisdom and fertility, and open books surmounted by foliage. Scholar Jonathan Lipman contends

The 1895 addition to the Oak Park house involved extending from the kitchen, on the eastern side of the building, and adding the delightful playroom (shown opposite) on the upper level. The fine skylights, sweeping arch of the ceiling, and harmonious use of natural brick and wood are among the features that show how Wright was beginning to develop new ideas. For his children the specially scaled windows and the *Arabian Nights* mural, which features a fisherman watching a genie rise from the magic lamp, made the room an enchanting place in which to play. The art-glass skylights and oak trim and furnishings distinguish the reception hall for the studio addition (above, in a view toward the drafting room).

that the design on the bas-reliefs is based partially on the ground plan of a section of the Roman Baths of Caracalla, constructed in AD 217. Wright's clients would be further impressed by the elegant name plaque set into the brickwork at the very entrance to the practice, with its distinctive device of a circle set within a square.

The house, built mainly of brick, oak, and glass, is remarkable for its innovative use of space. The living room, for example, has a continuous stringcourse at ceiling height, emphasizing the movement and flow of spaces, one into another, so that the walls take on the appearance of screens, with the doors and windows designed, as Wright himself put it, "as integral features of the structure and form, if possible its natural ornamentation."

The inscription on the fireplace reads:

TRUTH IS LIFE.

GOOD FRIEND, AROVND THESE
HEARTH-STONES SPEAK NO EVIL
WORD OF ANY CREATVRE · · ·

The focal point of the living room is a brick-built hearth with an inglenook—in Wright's term, "the sacred hearth," which he viewed as the heart of the home and family life. The hearth was to become a key feature of Wright's domestic architecture, sometimes forming the focal point of the whole design, as in the William H. Winslow House of 1893–94 in River Forest, Illinois. For this home, Wright was to design two central hearths, back to back, with an arcaded inglenook opening from the entrance hall and a smaller hearth forming the most prominent feature of the dining room that opens out from it.

Variations on the idea of the "sacred hearth" were to feature throughout his later domestic work and were often expressed on the exterior of the building by a prominent chimney.

At Oak Park, the Arts and Crafts-inspired motto "Truth is Life" carved above the fireplace emphasizes the status of the space, while the inglenook area was fitted with floor-length curtains that could be drawn across it to ensure greater privacy. The open flow of interior space around the central hearth includes the living room, dining room, and stair hall. The sense of a "total environment" is enhanced by the low ceiling and integrated seating, while the plain, leaded window glass provides a sense of privacy. The custom-designed, freestanding furniture is equally arresting, especially the large, extendable, oak dining table, surrounded by high-backed chairs of complex design, which were the precursors of many such dining ensembles in Wright's later work. The table is lit from above by the first of Wright's numerous light screens.

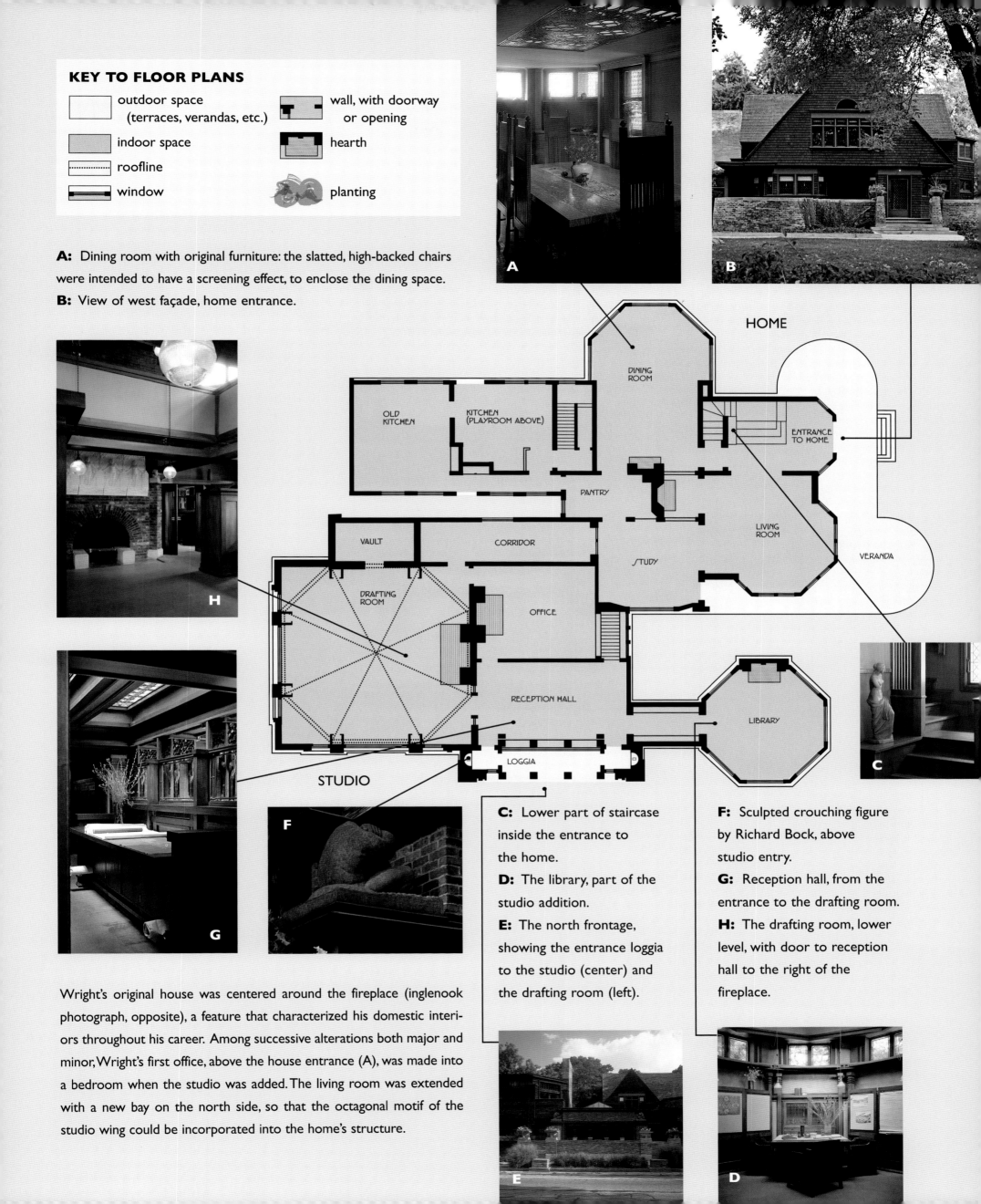

## KEY TO FLOOR PLANS

- ☐ outdoor space (terraces, verandas, etc.)
- ▨ indoor space
- ⋯ roofline
- ▭ window
- ▦ wall, with doorway or opening
- ▦ hearth
- 🪴 planting

**A:** Dining room with original furniture: the slatted, high-backed chairs were intended to have a screening effect, to enclose the dining space.

**B:** View of west façade, home entrance.

HOME

DINING ROOM

OLD KITCHEN

KITCHEN (PLAYROOM ABOVE)

ENTRANCE TO HOME

PANTRY

LIVING ROOM

VAULT

CORRIDOR

STUDY

VERANDA

DRAFTING ROOM

OFFICE

RECEPTION HALL

LIBRARY

LOGGIA

STUDIO

**C:** Lower part of staircase inside the entrance to the home.

**D:** The library, part of the studio addition.

**E:** The north frontage, showing the entrance loggia to the studio (center) and the drafting room (left).

**F:** Sculpted crouching figure by Richard Bock, above studio entry.

**G:** Reception hall, from the entrance to the drafting room.

**H:** The drafting room, lower level, with door to reception hall to the right of the fireplace.

Wright's original house was centered around the fireplace (inglenook photograph, opposite), a feature that characterized his domestic interiors throughout his career. Among successive alterations both major and minor, Wright's first office, above the house entrance (A), was made into a bedroom when the studio was added. The living room was extended with a new bay on the north side, so that the octagonal motif of the studio wing could be incorporated into the home's structure.

Wright usually showed his clients into his octagonal library (below) to review plans in a quieter environment than the busy studio drafting room. It is amply lit from above by the skylight and a series of windows set above the balcony, as well as pendant lamps. This room was doubtless a novel sight in suburban Oak Park, designed to make an impression on those who entered it. So, too, was the larger drafting room (opposite), the upper level of which is also octagonal, while its balcony is square-shaped, like the open workspace it overlooks. It is

suspended from the rafters on heavy-duty iron chains, which can be seen in the photograph opposite, taken from ground level. The drafting room has windows set between the structural beams to supplement the light from the clerestory. The space is unified by its simple brick and wood surfaces. To the right of the fireplace in the view opposite is the door to the reception hall; a sense of awe was created by the contrast between the relatively low-ceilinged entry and the height of the space it opens to, an effect that Wright repeated many times.

At the entrance to the studio (right), from Chicago Avenue, clients passed between square-shaped piers topped with planters and up toward Wright's elegantly carved name plaque (inset, below), above which crouched one of a pair of sculpted figures that were crafted by Richard Bock. The interplay of these decorative elements with the contrasting surfaces of brickwork and shingles, and the juxtaposition of triangular, square, and octagonal shapes, marked this out immediately as a center of creative and original design. Turning into the loggia and reception hall, visitors would notice the amber and green tones of the art-glass fixtures overhead (see page 23) and the built-in oak plan table, which forms a seamless part of the entrance hall's design. The library is on the right (the octagonal structure at the far side of the opposite page), while the drafting room is at left. In this unusual space, the solid square of the first story rises into an octagonal upper level (to the left of the chimney, main photo).

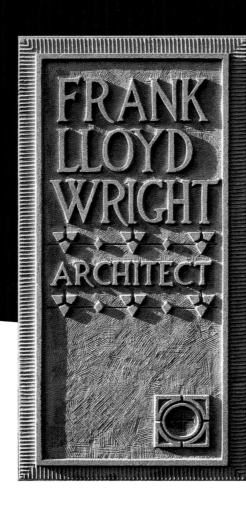

A new sense of spaciousness is apparent in the 15-foot-high (4.6-meter-high) barrel-vaulted playroom, which occupies the entire second floor of the new wing. Here the windows are the height of a child, so that grown-ups must stoop to look through them. Such an imaginative understanding of childhood extends to the overmantel, with its *Arabian Nights* mural and the child-scale stepped balcony. An art-glass skylight set in a fretwork, oak screen, brings extra light into the playroom, while the art-glass motifs are repeated in the built-in closet doors.

The use of glass is extraordinarily sophisticated throughout the interior working spaces of the showcase studio complex. The dramatic, paneled drafting room is ideally lit for its purpose by a skylight and bands of clear-glass windows. The spectacular design includes a balcony that is suspended on huge iron chains, forming an inward-looking working environment that makes impressive use of both engineering and the limited space of the site.

In the George Furbeck House (1897, above and right, after remodeling), in Oak Park, Wright repeated the octagon of his own studio in the corner towers and bay details. Inside, plain walls were trimmed with wood, and internal windows formed light screens. The nearby Rollin Furbeck House (opposite) was designed the same year for George's brother; both homes were wedding gifts from their father, Warren Furbeck. Historian Henry-Russell Hitchcock noted how Wright used vertical height to counterbalance the horizontal massing in Rollin's three-story home.

Art-glass sky-lights are used in the grand studio reception hall immediately beyond the impressive studio entrance loggia. The green, amber, and yellow panels help to maximize the relatively small space and provide a visual link between the drafting room, the library, and Wright's own office. The most elaborate art glass in the whole home-and-studio complex is the spectacular triptych of windows in Wright's secluded, top-lit office, which is set apart from the busy studio. Forming the focal point of the room, each of the windows frames the view through plate glass with an art-glass design of rectangles, bars, and squares. Wright's view that design should not compete with nature, but should complement it ("the view should stay severely put"), is at its most striking here. The semicircular sweep of the conservatory windows at the William H. Winslow House, with its curvilinear, framing designs, demonstrates a similar concept in this early period.

It is clear that Wright used his home and studio at Oak Park as a laboratory in which to experiment with his radical ideas.

As the center of his enterprise until he left Oak Park in 1909, an estimated 160 commissions, both public and private, were designed there. Wright made changes to both house and studio on a regular basis—at least half-yearly. Domestic commissions of the time, such as the Winslow House, with its simplification of forms and its interior spaciousness and sense of repose in particular, typically embody Wright's developing ideas of domestic space. That it is made to seem an integral part of its setting is also typical. Similarly, the long, low lines of the Frank Thomas (1901) and Ward W. Willits (1902–3) houses, among others, prefigure the next stage of Wright's career, and his dictum, "the horizontal line is the line of domesticity: shelter should be the essential look of any dwelling."

# "A YEARNING FOR SIMPLICITY"

◻ ◻ ◻

# The Prairie Style

◻ ◻ ◻

"My first feeling had been a yearning for simplicity ... Organic simplicity might be seen producing significant character in the harmonious order we call nature. Beauty in growing things. ... I loved the prairie by instinct as a great simplicity—the trees, flowers, sky itself, thrilling by contrast. I saw that a little height on the prairie was enough to look like much more—every detail as to height becoming intensely significant, breadths all falling short. ... I had an idea that the horizontal planes in buildings, those planes parallel to earth, identify themselves with the ground—make the building belong to the ground. I began putting this idea to work."

—*An Autobiography*

*Filtered sunlight streams through art glass into the tranquil living room of the Meyer May House (left), in Grand Rapids, Michigan.*

The Frank Thomas House (main picture, art-glass details above) conforms to an "L"-shaped plan, while most of the Prairie houses are
cruciform. Through the entry arch, a door can be glimpsed, but the
main floor is accessed by stairs concealed behind the high bounding
wall. Ever inventive with multilevel design, here Wright raised the
principal public rooms, freeing his clients from street-level intrusions
on their private living space.

# A /EN/E OF /HELTER

By 1900 Wright had designed some fifty structures, and his radical form of domestic architecture that later became known as
the Prairie style was beginning to evolve. "I saw the house primarily as liveable interior space under simple shelter," he wrote, in
*An Autobiography*, of the Prairie house and its place in the
sweeping Midwestern landscape. The appearance of a "sense of
shelter," as he defined it, was achieved by the way in which the
gently sloping or flat roof and the other "horizontal planes of the
building, those planes parallel to the earth, identify themselves
with the ground—make the building belong to the ground."

The characteristic long, low lines of the Prairie houses are
indeed intended to evoke the freedom and openness of the
prairie, although the sites on which they were built might in
some cases have been considered unpromising. Wright had
experimented with this idea in earlier Oak Park commissions,
but the Frank Thomas House (1901), considered the first
Prairie home in this suburb, marks a distinctive break with his
previous work, not least Wright's own studio's frontage on
Forest Avenue. As with other examples, including the imposing residence for Susan Lawrence Dana, the house stands on an
unprepossessing suburban site, leading Wright to focus
squarely on the "vista within." He achieved this by "breaking
the box": moving away from the traditional compartmental-
ization of living spaces and creating a total environment, with
the use of integrated natural materials, and particularly by
means of spectacular ensembles of art glass.

The continuous bands of art glass at the Frank Thomas House
reinforce the horizontality of the exterior, and the use of iridescent gold leaf in the distinctive arrow-headed window designs is
visible from the exterior. Wright had characteristically strong
views on the use of architectural glass, which, he wrote in 1928,
should always be a "shimmering fabric woven of rich glass—

patterned in color or stamped to form the
metal tracery—to be in itself a thing of delicate
beauty ... expressing the nature of that construction in the mathematics of the structure."

There is a distinct vertical emphasis to the asymmetrical William Fricke House (Oak Park, 1901, above), but signs of the emerging Prairie style are nevertheless apparent in the horizontal banding of the trim, the gentle inclines of the roof, and the generous over-hang of the eaves, whose undersides are light in color to "create a glow of reflected light that softly brightened the upper rooms." The intimate dining room is seen in the photograph at right.

In the deceptively low, two-story Prairie house built in Oak Park, in 1903, for Edwin H. and Mamah Borthwick Cheney (for whom Wright later left his wife), the bounding wall enclosing the courtyard garden provides privacy and the broad eaves, protec-tion from the elements, as seen in the snowbound scene below. No less than fifty-two art-glass windows bathe its restful inte-rior (living area, opposite) with soft, natural light.

The Frank Thomas House was much criticized for its "exotic" appearance at the time, and Wright was to spend almost a decade refining the ideas seen there, among which was a further integra-tion of the house and its site by means of a low bounding brick wall. One of the early examples of this use of a low wall between public and private spheres is at the Edwin H. Cheney House (1903), Oak Park, where Wright defines his "sense of 'wall' [as] no longer the side of a box. It was enclosure of space affording protection. … But it is also to bring the outside world into the house and let the inside of the house go outside."

Designed in 1902, the Ward W. Willits House in Highland Park, Illinois (shown in all photographs on these pages), is an early, but fully expressed, Prairie house. The living, dining (right), entrance, and service areas extend outward from the central hearth, all raised above ground level and amply illuminated with natural light; bedrooms (above) are on the upper level. William Storrer compares the transition through the contrasting entry and stairwell spaces (opposite, below) into the expansive living area (below) to a series of musical suspensions and tensions that resolve in perfect harmony.

# /TUDY IN /UMAC

Bringing the outside world inside in the case of the grandest and most opulent of the early Prairie houses, the Susan Lawrence Dana House, which was built in Springfield, Illinois, between 1902 and 1904, included the deployment of motifs drawn from such natural forms from the prairie as the sumac and countless butterflies. These can be traced throughout the house, not only in the detail of its construction, but in such decorative elements as the art glass and light fixtures. Wright later explained the use of such motifs as the sumac as both compensating for the lack of natural vegetation on the site and creating a unique, organic whole. "The differentiation of a single certain, simple form characterizes the expression of one building. Quite a different form may characterize another," he wrote.

Wright was given an unlimited budget and control of construction of the extravagant thirty-five-room mansion being built for the recently widowed heiress Susan Lawrence Dana. Her new residence—actually a total remodeling of the existing home—was designed primarily as a series of opulent spaces in which she could entertain her prestigious social circle, as well as house her considerable art collection. Located near the center of town and the state capitol, with the railroad running

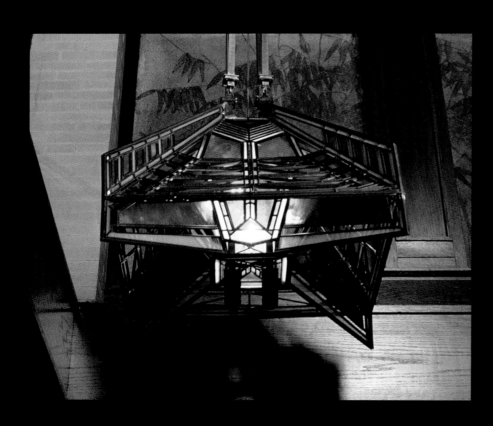

Art-glass lamps featuring an abstracted butterfly design (above) hang just above the dining table at the Susan Lawrence Dana House.

A figure sculpted by Richard Bock greets the visitor approaching the soaring, double-height reception hall, seen at right in a view from the living-room doors toward the loggia.

A

In the sumptuous Susan Lawrence Dana House, Wright extended his radical vision of multilevel design to new heights, so that rooms and openings flow one into another, forming a complex matrix in three dimensions. Both the reception hall and dining room rise to two stories, while the spectacular gallery/studio is double-height at the approach from the loggia, or walkway, but triple-storied at the far end, ascending from the library. The main entry is at street level; stairs skirt a tiled, open recess and lead up to the splendid reception hall. Harmonious tones and forms throughout enhance the rich beauty of the residence.

B

C

**A:** View from the north side of the gallery/studio, with the porch at the entrance to the kitchen and servants' dining room shown at left, and the loggia in the center.

**B:** View from the dining room toward the reception area.
**C:** The reception hall, looking toward the loggia.

G

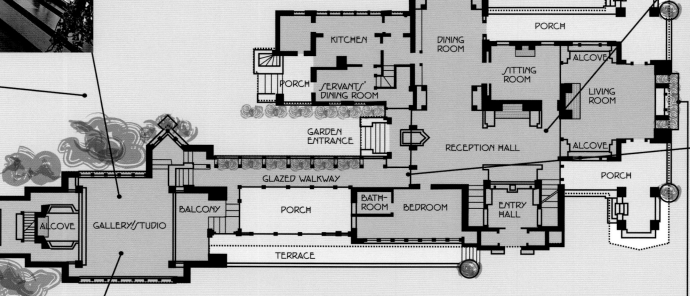

KITCHEN | DINING ROOM | PORCH
PORCH | SERVANTS' DINING ROOM | SITTING ROOM | ALCOVE
GARDEN ENTRANCE | LIVING ROOM
GLAZED WALKWAY | RECEPTION HALL | ALCOVE
ALCOVE | GALLERY/STUDIO | BALCONY | PORCH | BATH-ROOM | BEDROOM | ENTRY HALL | PORCH
TERRACE

D

**D:** The art-glass doors leading from the reception hall to the loggia.

F

E

**E:** The eastern façade, with the tripartite master-bedroom window at top and the living-room window below it.
**F:** View into the gallery/studio, facing south, from the balcony.
**G:** View into the gallery/studio, facing north.

along the rear edge, the site suggested a design that was focused on the interior and based on a series of vistas. The ceilings are of differing heights to introduce variety, while unexpected viewpoints add interest to different areas of social interaction and circulation, and the quintessentially Wrightian inglenook and stairwell transform the double-height entrance and reception area into a living hall. Throughout the design the "breaking of the box" is signified dramatically in the succession of spaces that each open into the other. The dining room is distinguished by the placing of the splendid dining table, sideboard, and tall-backed chairs in a grand, barrel-vaulted, basilicalike hall area with a breakfast alcove beyond, rather than as a separate "box" in the hierarchies of space conventionally observed in the traditional house plan.

The opening-up of the interior spaces can be read from the exterior elevation: a complex composition of distinctively toned Roman brick, stone copings, art-glass windows and doors, and roofs edged with copper. The overall rectilinear design is further embellished by a frieze that incorporates geometric forms and sumac motifs. In "In the Cause of Architecture," Wright later explained his use of the sumac motif, which appears in various forms throughout the house, particularly in the art-glass panels of the major rooms. Writing of his creation of such a total environment unique to each house, he explained: "Its grammar may be deduced from some plant form that has appealed to me, as certain properties in line and form of the sumach [sic] were used in the Lawrence house at Springfield." Fall colors further integrate the interior—gold, orange, and pale yellow predominate in the art glass, and the wood of the paneling and furniture throughout is autumnal red.

The grand residence, which soon became an important social and artistic focus for the area, took two years to complete. The use of glass is instrumental in creating a flow of light and opening up the interior throughout. Some 450 custom-made art-glass panels by Wright's favorite collaborator, the Linden Glass Company, exploit the decorative possibilities of the medium, from the iridescent fanlight of butterfly forms of the entrance arch—which appears amber and pale gold against the light from the interior, while reading green and blue from the outside in keeping with the cool tonalities of the exterior ornamentation—to the distinctive fall coloration of the windows of the great barrel-vaulted dining room. Here the sumac, the underlying motif of the whole house, is presented as paired abstractions of leaves, stems, and flowers, while the butterfly motif is taken up in the spectacular series of light fittings throughout the house, notably the magnificent hanging lamps designed by Wright for the dining room.

Abstracted butterflies in sun-kissed, golden hues are seen in the fanlight over the entrance, above (exterior views on page 43), in the arc of the porch's art-glass panel, and in reflection in the glazing of the inner door. The wings of the butterfly motif are reprised in the design for the pendant lamps suspended over the dining area (opposite). Despite the lofty expanse overhead and the lack of enclosing walls, a sense of convivial seclusion was created for dining guests by the high-backed dining chairs and the artful positioning of the hanging lamps. A subtle, sumac-inspired mural adorns the surrounding wall panels at balcony level.

The exterior views on page 43 illustrate the south façade (top; the gallery/studio is to the far left) and the entryway (below, left), whose piers and double fan of brickwork lend an unmistakable air of grandeur. The roofline detail (below, right) shows the flared edges of the copper eaves, revealing Wright's fondness for Japanese design, as well as the frieze, an echo of the architect's early days under Sullivan's tutelage.

"Go to the woods and fields for color schemes," wrote Wright, who favored "warm, optimistic tones of earth and autumn leaves," as seen in this luxury home's woodwork, furnishings, art glass, and decorative schemes. The windows shown above and below are variations on the sumac theme that recurs throughout the opulent building.

The window above is in the master bedroom, which is situated directly over the living room. The magnificent gallery/studio, opposite, is a freestanding hall attached to the main house by a glazed walkway leading from the entrance hall. Its unique fenestration fills the room with the diffused light that Wright—and his clients—so prized.

The Linden Glass Company, which was to work with Wright on Chicago's Midway Gardens and elsewhere, chose to feature in an advertisement in the *Architectural Record* in 1908 the art-glass doors and windows of another of the social spaces of the house, the triple-story gallery/studio. Here the grand ensemble of doors and windows employs motifs from pendant rather than upright sumac flowers and uses both opalescent and iridescent glass.

Wright's attention to detail is much in evidence throughout the house, from the almost life-sized terra-cotta statue, "Flower in the Crannied Wall," provided by Wright's long-term collaborator Richard Bock, and the fountain of the entrance hall to the copper urns, which were used as part of the overall design to provide geometric emphasis.

The warm, inviting tones of the Meyer May House's living-room woodwork and art-glass panels contrast with the wintry scene beyond (opposite). The exterior is of tan brick, with a red-tile roof (seen above from the southern end; the living room is at left). The elegant dining room, pictured below, features a mural in a subtle pastel palette by George Mann Niedecken, a carpet whose pattern echoes the art glass of the window design, and the acclaimed centerpiece dining set.

# A PRAIRIE DELIGHT

In the house built for Sophie and Meyer May (1908–10) in Grand Rapids, Michigan, the lighting schemes, whether free-standing or integral to the building, achieve further assimilation into the whole design. The design of the art-glass ceiling of the living room of the May residence, for example, is a sophisticated variation on a theme first seen above the Wrights' own dining table at Oak Park. In the Meyer May House, however, the artificial light is filtered not through rice paper but art glass, in subtle tones used elsewhere in the house and in the same geometric designs. The dining room has a notable range of leaded-glass windows and a fine mural, while the dining table itself, with its high-backed chairs (which symbolized to Wright the value of a contained and protective family unit), is here enhanced by four leaded art-glass lights whose posts are incorporated into the table itself. The ground plan of the house and its elevations differ from other Wright houses of the time. The dining and living rooms are ranged on either side of the entrance hall, while the brick living-room fireplace incorporates a feature that is unique in Wright's work. In an interesting development of the idea of the "sacred hearth," the horizontal joints of the masonry mortar sparkle with an iridescent light, even when no fire is blazing. In *An Autobiography*, Wright later noted: "It comforted me to see the fire burning deep in the solid masonry of the house itself."

# CONFETTI

Wright himself felt that the Avery Coonley House (1907–10) in Riverside, Illinois, was "the best that I could then do in terms of a house." Here the space was divided by function: the bedrooms and guest rooms each had separate wings around central living and dining spaces. Wright gave particular care to the decorative schemes throughout the house, few of which, alas, survive. The art-glass windows from the separate Avery Coonley Playhouse, completed in 1912, are, however, among Wright's most famous works and show him at his most playful in their abstract and radical design of balloons, confetti, and the American flag.

The stucco walls, windows, and decorated piers of the Avery Coonley House (above), viewed from the poolside terrace, on to which the original children's playroom looks. Directly over the playroom is the living room, a spacious expanse that rises tentlike into the hipped roof, with a hearth opposite the window wall that is seen here. Not to be confused with the playroom, the famous Avery Coonley Playhouse is a separate building dating from five years later. The original triptych of windows for which it is so well known is now at the Metropolitan Museum of Art in New York City, and a replica has been installed in the Playhouse itself.

The Isabel Roberts House (1908) in River Forest, Illinois, is shown on the opposite page. It was built on a cruciform plan, with the living room at one end of the main two-story axis, while the crosswing is a single story containing the dining room (at left on the exterior photograph opposite, above) and porch (at right). The living room (opposite, below) is distinguished by its tall windows (also seen in the exterior shot, above, center) and a balcony that overlooks the living space and garden. Underneath the balcony the room opens out on either side to the dining room and porch.

The Frederick C. Robie House's elevated main floor (above, right) is open plan, centering around the hearth and circumscribed by art glass rather than enclosing walls, bringing a serene, unfettered atmosphere to the apparently limitless living room. Further views are shown from the dining area toward the living room (page 53, top right) and of the living room from the hearth (pages 54–55).

# A VISTA WITHIN

Whereas some of the Prairie houses are spread over large, landscaped sites, the brick, steel, and limestone Frederick C. Robie House (1908–10) occupies a narrow city-corner lot. In its streamlined efficiency, the house appears to belong to a different world: the very materials of its construction immediately differentiate it from some of the earlier Prairie houses that were built from the cement stucco, wood, and tile that Wright deemed appropriate to their Midwestern sites. Plans of the house were published soon after it was finished and were to exert a huge influence on architects and designers, especially in Europe. Wright was gratified by the response to his revolutionary design, later writing that "the house became known in Germany as the *Dampfer* (ocean liner). This further emphasized that the machine could be a tool in the hands of an artist." The distinguishing features included the openness of its plan, the ship-like "prow," and the huge chimney, whose vertical emphasis balances the horizontal masses of the rest of the composition.

Wright's young client, Frederick C. Robie, who had trained as an engineer and was president of a bicycle-manufacturing company, had distinct ideas about the design of the house he commissioned for his growing family in suburban Chicago: he needed it to be fireproof and to afford privacy from his neighbors under a sheltering roof, yet he wanted open vistas within.

Viewed from the southwest corner (above), the superbly finished masonry (detail, page 55) and commanding roofline of the
Frederick C. Robie House form a protective barrier that
reveals scarcely a hint of the light-filled, airy living space inside.
The southern side of the main living space (with the sidewalk
running alongside in the photograph above) has a continuous
wall of art-glass doors, which can be seen to the left in the interior photograph on the opposite page, above right. Concealed
steel beams provide the structural support for what Robert
McCarter calls, in his 2006 biography of Frank Lloyd Wright, the
"exceptionally daring cantilevered roof overhangs to the east
and west." During the summer months, the extended eaves
serve to shade the interior from the heat of the sun. Wright
designed this so precisely that at midsummer, the sun just
touches the foot of the south-facing doors, while in midwinter,
its warming rays flood across the entire living-area floor, as
observed in 1969 by Reyner Banham.

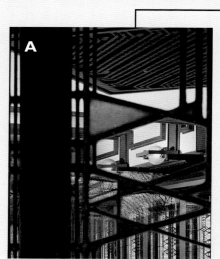

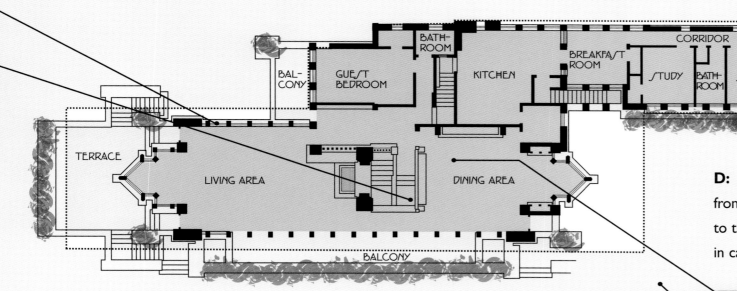

The plan of the main floor of the Frederick C. Robie House reveals that the living space is uninterrupted, except by the central hearth and stairwell that form the supporting core of the building.

**A:** Close-up detail of the art glass in the living area.

**B:** Looking southeast, from the stairwell to the main level.

**C:** The main and upper floors, from the southeast corner.

**D:** Looking toward the dining area from beside the hearth. The stairwell to the lower story is behind the built-in cabinet in the foreground.

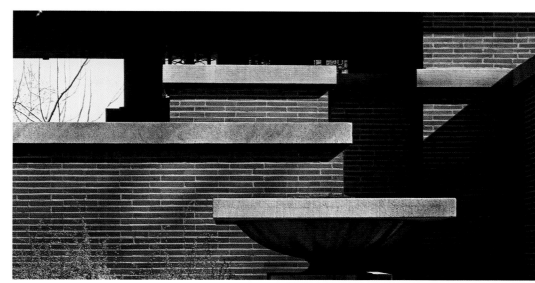

The sweeping horizontal planes of the exterior elevations, accentuated by the manner in which the bricks are laid, the limestone trims, the planters, and the broad-eaved roof give the house an extraordinary dynamism, unique in its time. The abstraction of forms so noticeable in the exterior is continued in the interior, and the specially designed furniture, wood and bronze light fixtures, and glass became hugely influential and part of the lexicon of twentieth-century architecture.

The design of the living room is radical in the extreme. Wright virtually disposed of interior walls and varied the ceiling heights around the central fireplace, while the leaded-glass windows and doors are continuous around the space, forming a shimmering screen that appears to dissolve the materials of the building, giving an extraordinary sense of subtle elegance and repose.

A photograph of the dining room soon after it was completed in 1910 shows the integration of every element of the design into a total environment. Wright's controlling instinct extended even to the designs of the dresses worn by Catherine, his first wife, in early photographs. In the image of the dining room, the rectilinear motifs of tables, chairs, built-in sideboard, art-glass windows, and carpet patterns are in geometric contrast to the bronze and glass globes of the light fixtures forming the terminal points of the wooden panels running across the ceiling. Originally, the four corners of the dining table were illuminated by built-in lamps, whose art-glass shades reflected the design of the windows. Wright's desire that light fixtures should be "made a part of the building … no longer an appliance, nor even an appurtenance, but really architecture" may be said to have reached its culmination here.

Wright later observed that "This absorbing, consuming phase of my experience as an architect ended about 1909." He traveled to Berlin, Germany, to assist in the publication of his work in portfolio form. Leaving his wife and their six children, he closed the studio at Oak Park, handing over his design projects for others to complete, and a new phase in his work began.

# "THREE TIMES BUILT, TWICE DESTROYED, AND YET A PLACE OF GREAT REPOSE"

◩ ◩ ◩

## Taliesin

◩ ◩ ◩

"Taliesin is a natural building, in love with the ground, built of native limestone quarried nearby. Sand from the river below was the body of its plastered surfaces, plain wood slabs and marking strips of red cypress finish the edges, mark the ceilings, and make the doors and sash. … Any modern building really out of the ground is timeless."

—*Architectural Forum,* January 1938
(in *Collected Writings,* Vol. 3)

*The great rectangular living room in Taliesin III (left), looking back toward the central fireplace, screens, and bookshelf seat that disguise the entrance from the view of occupants relaxing in this part of the house.*

Taliesin, the home and studio that Wright originally built for himself and his lover, Mamah Borthwick Cheney, in 1911 near Spring Green, Wisconsin, after their return from Europe, was erected on a site of intense personal significance for Wright, and remained intimately—and tragically—interwoven with his private and professional concerns throughout the rest of his long life. Due to a series of major fires, the complex developed in three phases, designated Taliesin I (1911), Taliesin II (1914), and Taliesin III (1925). Sometimes called Taliesin East to distinguish it from its desert offspring, Taliesin West (1937), it underwent further modifications after yet another fire, at the Hillside Home School, in 1952. In each case except the last, however, it was mainly the living space that was damaged and rebuilt.

# A HILLSIDE HOME

The Cheneys had been neighbors of the Wrights in Oak Park, Illinois, where Wright and his first wife, Catherine, were raising their six children, and Wright had designed a house for them (the Edwin H. Cheney House: see pages 36–37) in 1903. In 1909 Wright and Mrs. Cheney fled their respective marriages and, in the face of Catherine's refusal to divorce Wright, took refuge in Europe, leaving his Chicago practice in considerable confusion. On their return Wright was determined to make a new start and decided, as he wrote in his *An Autobiography*, to transfer "Work, life and love … to the beloved ancestral Valley where my mother … had bought the low hill on which Taliesin now stands and she offered it to me now as a refuge."

The "ancestral Valley" was Hillside, near Spring Green in Wisconsin, where Wright's Welsh grandparents, the pioneering Lloyd Jones family, had first settled during the 1860s, and where four of his uncles had established farms and two of his aunts had founded the progressive Hillside Home School. Wright had spent vacations working on the farms and had designed his first built work, a new school building (the Hillside Home School Building), for his aunts in 1887; as well as the Romeo and Juliet Windmill Tower in 1896; a new building for the Hillside Home School from 1901 to 1903; and a Prairie house, "Tan-y-deri," for his sister, Jane, and her husband, Andrew Porter, in 1907; the idea of returning to this loved and familiar place must have been hugely appealing.

"Taliesin," the name of a mythical Welsh poet, means "shining brow" in Welsh, and in Wright's final plan, dated June 1911, the wings of his new home—one for the living quarters and a longer one for the studio—wrapped themselves around the sides of the hill rather than crowning it, becoming, as Wright later wrote, "the brow of the hill." The living quarters were based on the

Taliesin III viewed from across the pond (above); the projecting birdwalk emphasizes the integral relationship between the complex and its rural setting.

Wright's Romeo and Juliet Windmill Tower (left) was erected at Hillside in 1896 to pump water for use by the Hillside Home School that his aunts ran. The diamond-shaped and octagonal tower segments together represent the Shakespearean lovers locked in a supportive embrace. The original structure was completely renovated in 1992.

Wright designed a series of gardens to form a harmonious whole with the house's stone piers, parapets, and shingled roofs (above).

As the Taliesin Fellowship grew and flourished, Wright converted the nearby Midway Barns (left) for use by the community. Crops of alfalfa, soybeans, corn, wheat, and other grains were planted in rotation, tended by the apprentices, from 1938. Wright himself had helped out on his uncles' farms near Spring Green during his boyhood summers.

Prairie-house paradigm, but with the backyard at the front. The wide, "U"-shaped courtyard formed by the wings opened up the whole structure to the hill behind, signaling a close connection between house and landscape that was new in Wright's work, and that was to become one of the most radical and recognizable features of his later creations. "Unthinkable to me, at least unbearable," Wright wrote in his autobiography, "that any house should be put *on* that beloved hill … It should be *of* the hill. Belonging to it. Hill and house should live together each the happier for the other … Now I wanted a *natural* house to live in myself."

A further novelty was the combination of living, working, and agricultural space: at the end of the studio wing, Wright sited a farmyard with wagon shed and horse stalls, describing in his autobiography how he intended Taliesin to be "self-sustaining, if not self-sufficient …" providing "shelter, food, clothes and even entertainment within itself." Here, at this early point, he was already flagging the ideas that underlay the Taliesin Fellowship that he founded with his third wife, Olgivanna, nearly twenty years later.

# STONE AND WOOD

Taliesin was constructed largely of local stone, like the Hillside Home School annex building of 1901–3, and with massive piers that seemed to grow out of the ground. With their horizontal lines, low-slung, deeply overhanging, pitched roofs, freestanding piers, and ribbon windows, the living quarters share many of the characteristics of the Prairie houses, but also mark a new independence from the principles of Classical symmetry underlying much of Wright's earlier work. The local limestone used for the piers, the great chimneys, and the lower walls was laid in a random pattern of loosely projecting layers, creating a textured surface very different from the smooth ashlar of the Hillside Home School. Upper wall surfaces were roughly stuccoed with long bands of plaster made from the yellowish Wisconsin sand, and were framed above and below by molded wooden strings. The complicated, many-layered roof was the most conspicuous feature, with gable elements and penthouses among the prominent hips, and the whole covered with shingles left to weather to silver-gray "like the tree branches spreading below them." The effect is solid, natural: "Taliesin was to be an abstract combination of stone and wood as they naturally met in the aspect of the hills around about," as Wright explained in his *An Autobiography*.

The overall plan was equally informal and irregular, with each wing being loosely organized and the rooms opening into each other at the corners, creating long, diagonal lines of sight both through the building and out, on to the hillside. The wings were linked in a wandering pattern that looped around the hill, following its natural contours, and the living and studio areas were separated by an open loggia aligned with the entrance driveway, so that the hill seemed to look through the house. The large, rectangular living room sat in the angle of the loggia and the dining terrace and extended out into space, offering a sequence of vistas that finally opened out into a 270-degree panorama across the river valley to the hills beyond as the visitor negotiated the great fireplace that blocked the immediate view.

In its ambitious scale and concern with the landscaping of both house and grounds, Taliesin has more in common with the great Italian country estates that Wright and Mamah had visited during their stay in Fiesole than with any of Wright's previous designs, as Neil Levine has shown. Its hillside setting is reminiscent of Roman and Florentine villas, and, as part of his final plan, Wright designed a formal garden, a terraced garden, a vegetable garden, and a wild garden, following Italian principles to effect a slow transition from the living space to the working agricultural lands beyond. Water formed an integral part of the design: Wright dammed the stream at the foot of the hill to make a water

The gardens are alive with the sound of running water and enriched by Wright's collection of Eastern artworks, including a great Buddha (these pages; opposite, Taliesin I, the Hilltop courtyard; above, steps leading to Wright's residence). In *An Autobiography,* he describes an idyllic existence with Olgivanna and the children, "Up at sunrise this late September morning walking in the thick blue-grass, bare feet in the thick white rime of frosty dew."

garden, and used the power of the waterfall thus created to channel the water in a series of ornamental streams and fountains.

Partway down the entrance slope, Wright placed a flight of steps and, at their foot, positioned a cast of the sculpture that he had designed (sculpted by Richard Bock) for the Susan Lawrence Dana House (1902–4), in Springfield, Illinois, "Flower in the Crannied Wall," the muse of architecture being shown as a stylized, but sensuous, female figure delicately building a tower out of geometric building blocks. In the Dana House, she had been positioned within the entrance, marking the point where nature gave way to architecture. Her position well down the garden at

Taliesin is suggestive of Wright's by now much wider ambitions.

The Hungarian-American photographer and architect Balthazar Korab, whose images illustrate the pages of this book, visited Taliesin in the summer of 1958 and recorded the powerful impression that the place made on him; his article was reprinted in 1993 in the *Journal of the Taliesin Fellows.* "Evening sun rested over Taliesin when we drove up last summer; elegance and peace … There are places that express unmistakably the life and thoughts of their masters … Mont St. Michel, Les Baux, and Taliesin East are such places."

# FIRE AND LOSS

From its inception Taliesin was intended to be the center of Wright's life and work, and the focus of the collaborative lifestyle that he and Mamah Borthwick Cheney had developed during their time abroad, and, as such, it underwent a constant process of change and development. The early years after their return were hard, for the scandal of their liaison initially deterred commissions, but they gradually settled back into life in Chicago at a time when literary and artistic life was flowering into the "Chicago Renaissance," and when commercial and government clients were starting to show an interest in the Prairie school. Major commissions came for the Midway Gardens (1913), in Chicago, and the Imperial Hotel (1913–23), in Tokyo, Japan, but even prior to those Wright had begun to plan for the expansion of the office and studio section of Taliesin. This was to include a two-story addition to the workroom and dormitory space for the growing number of draftsmen, although this last was not built until the 1920s.

The first, and by far the most appalling, of the series of conflagrations that dogged the history of Taliesin occurred in 1914. On August 15, while Wright was in Chicago, a disaffected and disturbed domestic employee set fire to the house, destroying the living quarters, and attacked the residents with a hatchet, killing Mamah, her two children (who were visiting), and four of Wright's draftsmen. Wright was totally devastated, and although he almost immediately announced his intention of rebuilding the house, did not live there again on anything like a settled basis for the next fifteen years. The rebuilding followed much the same design as for Taliesin I, but Wright noted that he made one significant change from the original: a loggia, which he aligned with the "Flower in the Crannied Wall" sculpture, and which looked up the valley to the family chapel, where Mamah was buried.

Further expansion of Taliesin during the 1920s saw additional provision for draftsmen and workmen living on the estate, but in 1925 disaster struck again with a second fire, caused this time by faulty wiring, destroying the living quarters. The timing was bad on many counts: Wright was still in debt as a result of the first rebuilding; his second marriage, to Miriam Noel, had collapsed and he was being pursued by her lawyers—at one point she even had him arrested and jailed; and his new love, Olgivanna Lazovich (who became the third Mrs. Wright in 1928), was sued by her ex-husband in 1926 for custody of their daughter. Wright even lost Taliesin for a time, when the bank foreclosed on his debts and remunerative work was in short supply. It was a bleak period for him, and the only way he found to save Taliesin was to incorporate his practice and sell shares in his potential earning power to wealthy friends. But the Wall Street Crash of 1929 was a further blow, and it was well into the 1930s before Wright's career recovered from this series of setbacks.

Apprentices at Taliesin gathered for musical and theatrical evenings in the Hillside Theater (1952, left) and the music room (opposite). Triangular trusses above the desks in the drafting room at the former Hillside Home School buildings (above). "Taliesin scenes are homely scenes," said Wright in *An Autobiography*.

# CHANGE AND RENEWAL

The proposal in 1928 to incorporate Wright's practice as the Taliesin Fellowship also marked the beginning of the extraordinary school of architecture that grew up around him. For years Wright had been approached by young people who were keen to come and work with him as apprentices, and the arrangement was made more formal when a group of them started living and working at Taliesin under Wright's supervision in return for a fee. In 1932 the Fellowship was formed. This in turn changed Wright's working practices: he came to rely on the apprentices and ceased employing draftsmen. And it also changed Taliesin, which underwent a constant process of enlargement and modification right up to Wright's death, in order to accommodate both the working and the social space that such an enlarged group required.

Thus the program of renewal at Taliesin after the Fellowship was formed was an opportunity to enlarge it for its new purpose. The old Hillside Home School buildings were renovated and a drafting room was created, with eight apprentice rooms along each side. The roof was formed of oak trusses with clerestory windows so that light fell on the drafting tables. In 1933 a playhouse was added to the complex, which was rebuilt after the fire of 1952 as the Hillside Theater. A collection of buildings halfway between Hillside and Taliesin, the Midway Barns, were converted in 1938 into a granary, stables, dairy, and machine shed, and the fields around were planted with rotating crops with which to feed the community.

Life at Taliesin was physically demanding: the apprentices not only provided the labor for Wright's building projects in addition to their studies, but were also responsible for the house and farm work. There was, however, a lighter side. Wright describes in his autobiography the Saturday and Sunday evening gatherings, "for supper and a concert, or a reading ... always happy, always fresh—not only composed of perfectly good material, good music, good food, enthusiastic young people, good company, but something rare and fine was in the air of these homely events."

Balthazar Korab gives an elegiac description of a similar scene that he witnessed during his visit in 1958:

> But Taliesin was living. Living just one of its routine days; the farmworkers were gathering in for dinner, some musician stopped his practice, five-continent-company lined up for the showdown of those who prepared dinner that night. An air of joyous activity pervaded the picture, similar to some medieval illumination, where all trade and commerce figure on an area the size of a matchbox;—or a Breughel painting. The hilly site helps to build up this view—the school, the master's house, the farm; each occupies its own hill, grouped in a triangle, scattered with single oaks and cedar-like pines.
>
> Only the "Residence" hill is enveloped richly in dark green, mirrored in the most peaceful of the lakes. Approaching next morning I felt, rather than saw, that something grew there behind, and together with the oaks and vines; organic architecture, flashed the thought, profanely, categorizing where the air commended.

# "PERMANENT, NOBLE, BEAUTIFUL"

◧ ◧ ◧

## "California Romanza" and the Textile-block Houses

◧ ◧ ◧

"The concrete block ... might be permanent, noble, beautiful. ... Concrete is a plastic material—susceptible to the impress of imagination. I saw a kind of weaving coming out of it. Why not weave a kind of building? ... Lightness and strength! Steel the spider spinning a web within the cheap plastic material wedded to it by pouring an inner core of cement after the blocks were set up. The 'shell' as human habitation. Why not? Another phase of architecture organic. The straight line, the flat plane, now textured. The sense of interior space coming through, the openings all woven together as integral features of the shell. ... Decoration asserts the whole to be greater than any part and succeeds to the degree that it helps make this good."

—*An Autobiography*

*The patterned south façade of the Charles Ennis House (left).*

In *An Autobiography*, Wright describes his radical use of the concrete block at the Alice Millard House (1923–24) thus: "We would take that despised outcast of the building industry the concrete block—out from underfoot or from the gutter—find a hitherto unsuspected soul in it—make it live as a thing of beauty—textured like the trees."

Wright had worked with concrete previously, notably in the Unity Temple (see pages 138–41), for which the concrete was cast in place. His experiments with the material continued during the construction of the Imperial Hotel (1913–23), Tokyo, Japan—the "jointed monolith," which Wright worked upon at the same time as his developing California plans, traveling between the two places and conducting much of his negotiations with his client Aline Barnsdall by correspondence until his return from Japan in 1922.

Wright's long-standing admiration for Japanese art and architecture was profound, and its influence upon him, great. His status worldwide was hugely enhanced in 1923, when the Imperial Hotel remained virtually undamaged after the strongest earthquake in Japanese history struck. Wright had conceived the hotel as a "flexible structure," with concrete as a crucial component, and so the grand construction had the flexibility to sustain great pressure: what Wright termed "the ability to push and pull on a building."

He was also aware of concrete's historical importance as a building material, including in Roman times—the Colosseum and the dome of the Pantheon in Rome, Italy, are made of concrete. Skilled labor was not required, so it could be used for buildings and engineering structures throughout the Roman Empire, using whatever material was available locally for the mix.

A view from the east side into the courtyard of the Aline Barnsdall House, looking over the circular pool (opposite). The loggia at the end of the courtyard leads into the living room. Behind the ornamented row of piers at right are the dining and kitchen spaces.

Wright's aerial perspective of his "California Romanza" (above) shows the house from the west, with the ornamental pool off the living room in the foreground and the walkway leading to the entrance in the center ground, at left. The hilltop site attracts cooling breezes and commands stunning views of the Hollywood Hills to the north.

For Wright this flexibility of use, and the fact that the raw materials of the specific locale literally became an organic part of the building, were crucial. He writes in *An Autobiography*, "all we have to do is educate the concrete block, refine it and knit it together with steel in the joints and so construct the joints that they could be poured full of concrete. The walls would thus become thin but solid reinforced slabs and yield to any desire for form imaginable. And common labor could do it all." He furthermore stressed, "concrete is a plastic material—susceptible to the impressions of the imagination."

# ROMANCE

Always eager to distance himself from European-based, historicizing styles, and passionate in his desire to embrace regionalism, Wright wanted to create something uniquely Californian when he designed a house-and-theater complex in an olive grove high upon a hill in Hollywood, California, for the heiress Aline Barnsdall, who purchased the site in 1919. He had met his client some years earlier; in his autobiography he described her as "a pioneer," living up to "the integral romance when all about her was ill with pseudo-romantic in terms of neo-Spanish, lingering along as quasi Italian, stale with Renaissance or dead of English half-timber and colonial." In *A Testament* (1957), he wrote: "Architecture is truly romantic.

There should lie in the very science and poetry of structure the inspired love of Nature. This is what we should and do now call Romantic." Calling this work "California Romanza," Wright's design for the ambitious complex drew both on his client's wishes (conveyed in part by correspondence) and on his interpretation of the site and its cultural antecedents, including pre-Columbian forms.

The Aline Barnsdall House (1917–21) is essentially a courtyard structure turning in on patios cooled by plantings and water features, with a series of art-glass folding (later changed to sliding) doors and windows serving to further the apparent dissolution of the house into its surroundings. The dreamlike quality of the house recalls Mayan temples in its monolithic shapes. Abstracted forms of the hollyhock, Aline Barnsdall's favorite flower, provide the dominant motifs throughout the house, from the exterior elevations, where a decorative horizontal frieze adds texture to the otherwise plain, gently sloping walls, and the piers and columns, to the interior decoration. The custom-designed carpets and high-backed chairs, sofa tables, and specially designed sofa lamps are all adorned with such forms. The furnishings and motifs are finished in a distinctive hollyhock theme throughout the house, and the scheme is seen to particularly fine effect in the living-room skylight, in which patterned and clear glass are interspersed; in the play-porch windows and door for Aline Barnsdall's small daughter; and in the run of

floor-to-ceiling windows of the master bedroom. Abstract "art-stone" concrete ornamentation is also used to harmonious effect in the living-room fireplace, which is reflected in a shallow pool before it. Wright employs the four elements at this hearth (pictured on the opposite page): earth, in the stonework; air, or light, from the art-glass skylight above; fire; and water, in the hearthside pool, in this, the most theatrical of his domestic spaces.

Hollyhock-inspired furnishings in the dining room of the Aline Barnsdall House (above). The living room (opposite) is dominated by its fireplace and the built-in furniture, which is seen in the foreground (a light pier is at right, adjoining the rear side of the sofa). From the exterior, the apparently unbroken, flat planes of the walls suggest a dimly lit interior, but tall windows are set beneath the level of the frieze, behind ornamented piers, so that plenty of light is filtered into the open rooms within, yet the harsh glare of the southern Californian sun is kept at bay. Above the living-room fireplace is the only example in a Wright house of a skylight over a hearth.

# TEXTILE BLOCKS

During the construction of "Hollyhock House," and building on the experience he had gained in Japan, Wright developed a new method of building with concrete, which he called his "textile-block" system. He cast in molds blocks of concrete, reinforced with steel, patterning the blocks so that the humble "gutter-rat" could be transformed into an attractive material. The blocks were grooved at the edges and could be laid up together, bound by steel rods positioned vertically and horizontally in the grooves, and grouted with poured concrete, to hold the entire structure firm—and all without requiring specialized expertise.

The use of textile blocks had the further advantage of providing Wright with hitherto undreamed-of possibilities of creating light and shade in the strong Californian sunshine, because the blocks could be pierced—with or without glazing—as well as patterned. The perforated blocks filter light to create exciting shadows in the interior, while providing privacy—the all-essential "sense of shelter," in Wrightian terms. Conversely, when seen lit from within, they provide dramatic emphasis to the exterior at night.

"La Miniatura" (1923–24) in Pasadena, the house designed for Alice Millard, was the first of four Californian concrete-block houses. It was followed by his three textile-block houses: a Hollywood residence for John Storer (1923–25) and hillside homes of 1924–25 for Harriet and Samuel Freeman and Mabel and Charles Ennis, both in Los Angeles. The compact house that was built on a steep site for the Freemans was based on a block embellished with an abstract design and used for solid, perforated, and glazed areas alike. The perforated and glazed blocks are used to form contrasts to the extensive plain glazed areas—a variation on Wright's abiding concept of the glass screen—in the living-room windows that look down upon Los Angeles.

While the Samuel Freeman House is designed to appear an integral part of its site, the symmetrical "T" plan and double-height block of the John Storer House, with its central section containing the living and dining room, are offset by a series of terraces on its sloping site. The dramatic living area opens on to the upper terrace, while, as at the Millard and Barnsdall houses, the fireplace is placed asymmetrically, although here the inglenook is situated along one side only of the "sacred hearth."

Wright's long-term fascination with America's pre-Columbian past, seen in several of his California projects, perhaps reached its culmination in the design and siting of the Charles Ennis House in the hills above Los Feliz. The textile block used for this monumental home could be said to have created its own spatial lexicon, taking its motif from the block itself. This can be seen in the exterior design, particularly in the primary, south-facing,

The light from a series of full-height windows throws the patterned interior blocks into decorative relief in the John Storer House (1923–25) living room (opposite). The terrace doors at the far end backlight the perforated "screen" that frames the seating area before the fireplace. Wright's barrel chairs are seen in the foreground, right.

Inside the Charles Ennis House (above), spaces are defined by the rhythmic, modular arrangement of both plain and patterned blocks. The repeating overlapping-squares pattern, seen in the foreground detail, directs the eye diagonally upward.

**A:** Exterior textile-blocks detail.

**B:** The east façade, with a bedroom leading to a terrace.

**C:** Art-glass doors between the bedroom and living area.

**D:** The north façade; the entrance is at right, under the bridge.

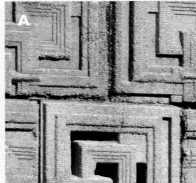

Wright's son Lloyd supervised construction of the Ennis House, which, due to its sheer scale and other structural factors, was to prove difficult to maintain. Extensive renovations were undertaken by subsequent owners, and the Ennis House Foundation began a major rehabilitation program of stabilization and restoration in 2005. The simple, linear plan translates to three dimensions as a complex matrix of interlocking volumes. It is evident from the expansive terraces that the original client wanted as much outdoor space as indoor.

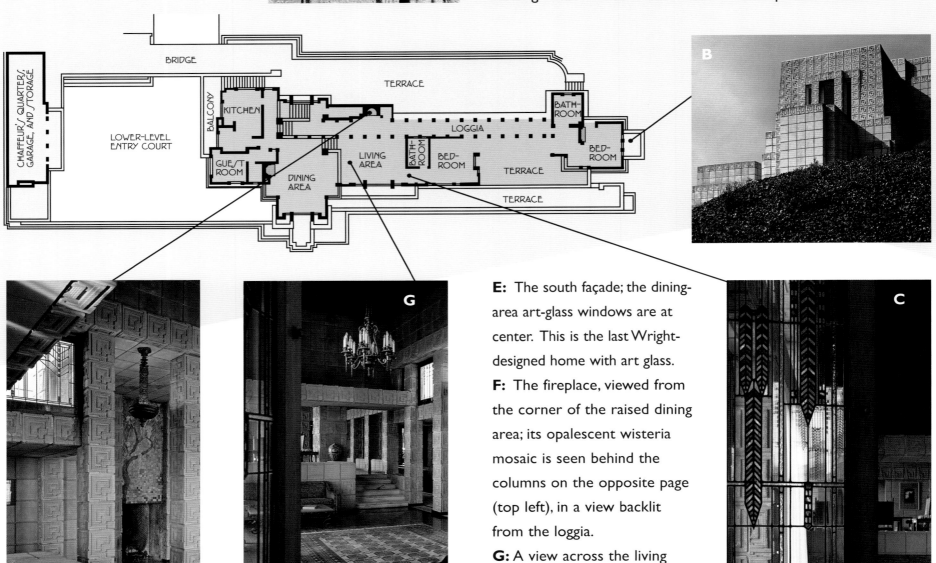

**E:** The south façade; the dining-area art-glass windows are at center. This is the last Wright-designed home with art glass.

**F:** The fireplace, viewed from the corner of the raised dining area; its opalescent wisteria mosaic is seen behind the columns on the opposite page (top left), in a view backlit from the loggia.

**G:** A view across the living area toward the steps to the dining area.

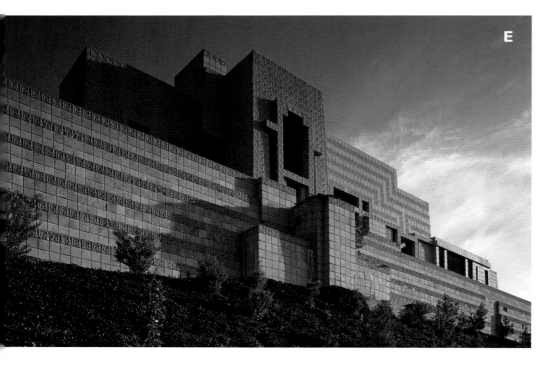

citadel-like elevation set on the very summit of the steeply sloping mountain ridge. It is one of Wright's most eclectic and futuristic designs—a status confirmed by its use in British movie director Ridley Scott's iconic *Blade Runner* (1982), which was completed nearly sixty years after the house was built. At the time of building, Wright himself was characteristically confident of its future: writing to Charles and Mabel Ennis in 1924, he stated: "You see, the final result is going to stand on that hill a hundred years or more. Long after we are gone it will be pointed out as the Ennis House, and pilgrimages will be made to it by lovers of the beautiful—from everywhere."

At 10,000 square feet (930 square meters), the Ennis House is the largest of the textile-block houses, and the last of Wright's houses to employ art glass. The main dining room commands a spectacular view of Los Angeles, a view that Wright frames in a triptych of windows that is reminiscent, on a huge scale, of the windows in his own study at his home-and-studio complex at Oak Park. Here, too, in its abstract, framing forms, are expressed Wright's characteristically trenchant views on windows, explained in a 1928 essay (published in *In the Cause of Architecture*): "Nothing is more annoying to me than any tendency of realism of form in window glass, to get mixed up with the view outside. A window pattern should stay severely 'put.'"

The diagonal forms of the design are pure abstractions in a blue/green palette, with subtle variations in the width of the caming. Opalescent and iridescent glass is used in the mosaic overmantel of the dramatic colonnade. The curvilinear forms of the wisteria motif (seen above), and the distinctive coloration of the blossoms against a gold, silver, and bronze background, are set in counterpoint to the austere squares-within-squares of the block designs.

Wright intended the California houses to be an appropriate response to their location in both form and function. The textile block might, as he wrote in *An Autobiography*, "be fit for a phase of modern architecture. It might be permanent, noble, beautiful. It would be cheap." However, Wright's radical dwellings did not find general favor in southern California. Twenty-five years later he was to adapt, refine, and simplify the concept for a different world, in the shape of the "Usonian automatic."

# "THE TRULY MODERN HOUSE"

## Usonian Houses

"Suppose, then, we consider briefly a much broader application of the principles of an organic architecture: the moderate house for the citizen in moderate circumstances. ... What, then, is desirable to this new house? ... [F]ree association with considerably more ground than the old house ... sunlight and vista, a spaciousness ... privacy ... a free pattern for the occupation of the family that is to live in the house. ... It would be ideal to have all these requirements meet in some integral harmony of proportion to the human figure; to have all details so designed as to make the human relationship to the building not only convenient but charming. ... There must also be beauty—beauty of which man himself is capable. ... I have been describing here a particular house, the house of Herbert Jacobs built at Madison, Wisconsin."

—*Architecture and Modern Life*, 1937
(in *Collected Writings*, Vol. 3)

*The generous, warmly lit windows and mellow timber of the post-war Melvyn Maxwell Smith House (left)—a typically Usonian construction with an "L"-shaped floor plan—form a comforting contrast to the winter scenery.*

Wright's lifelong ability to respond to changing social and economic needs, as well as his continuing capacity to reinvent both himself and his idea of an organic architecture, yet remain true to his fundamental principles, are apparent in the remarkable achievements that date from the last quarter-century of his career. Meeting challenges both professional and personal, from the early 1930s he found fresh inspiration that enabled his creativity to flourish, so that his output blossomed in terms of excellence, virtuosity, and sheer quantity during a time of life that is rarely characterized by such a trajectory. Wright was always attuned to the need for architecture that is appropriate to its site, its temporal and social context, and the needs and desires of its intended occupants. The renewal of his fortunes and creative energies during this period was expressed not only in his most famous and iconic structures, like Fallingwater (1935–37), in Bear Run, Pennsylvania, and New York's Solomon R. Guggenheim Museum (1943–59), but also in his Usonian houses, which redefined domestic design in accordance with his organic principles, and in ways that are still relevant to—and manifest in—the homes that we live in today.

# WRIGHT REBORN

After the stock-market crash of 1929 and the Great Depression that followed, Wright was forced to shift his focus. There was an urgent need for economically designed housing for middle- and lower-income families, and the solutions that he found in what he termed the "Usonian house," for clients working within a limited budget, were key contributions to the domestic architecture of the twentieth century. In conjunction with his world-famous masterpieces, these new houses were also a considerable factor in the rescue of his reputation, which, since the early decades of the century, had been adversely affected by the scandals and tragedy of his personal life.

Wright used the term "Usonian," generally understood to mean "of the United States," as early as 1925, although the meaning came to be adapted to different uses over time, incorporating, according to various claims, concepts ranging from usefulness to universality and even Utopia. Wright himself was later to use it to include more than one hundred houses on sites across North America, from the Great Lakes to the Pacific Northwest region, which were constructed to his

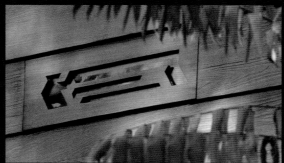

The Gregor Affleck House in Bloomfield Hills, Michigan (1940, these pages), represents a significant link between the ideas developed by Wright in his Broadacre City project and his fully fledged Usonian houses. The concept for the house is taken from the Broadacre City model of a "house for sloping ground"; sited on a wooded hillside, its sunroom and sleeping quarters rest on the ground, while the living/dining space is cantilevered out over the slope, with the balcony a half-story lower. The plan is the Usonian "L" shape, and the main material is local cypress, now weathered in places to a warm gray.

own designs, the process often being supervised by apprentices from the Taliesin Fellowship, which he founded in 1932.

The architect had consistently sought a "democratic" architecture, which was articulated in his plans for a decentralized community that was not overcrowded, dehumanized, or soulless, as he feared cities were becoming, but rather open, spacious, and connected to the land. He named his ideal community Broadacre City (1934–35), but it was only ever realized in scale-model form. The ideas behind it were explained in his book *The Disappearing City* (1932), in which he lamented that the constant motion of city life "robs the urban individual of the meditation, imaginative reflection and projection once his as he lived and walked under clean sky among the growing greenery to which he was born companion." Each family, he believed, should have its own acre to call home. While Wright's city was never built, the inexpensive, utilitarian, yet beautifully designed Usonian house was greatly influenced by this project.

The 1936 home built for Herbert Jacobs in Madison, Wisconsin, for $5500 (including the architect's fee) is generally recognized as the first of Wright's Usonian houses, but the Malcolm Willey House (1934), in Minneapolis, Minnesota, is a significant precursor in many ways. The Willeys approached Wright for a design at a time when business was slow and the cost of running Taliesin was a major burden on him. They were apparently pleasantly surprised when the famous architect accepted the commission for a modest, middle-class home in Minneapolis. As with many of the later Usonian designs (and, indeed, with some of Wright's more prestigious work), the swift establishment of a friendly personal connection between architect and client was an important factor. Malcolm Willey was an academic and sociologist, and had authored a recent report recommending electronic and transport policies geared to a dispersed population, ideas that chimed very well with Wright's Broadacre City concept. The Willey House as built is a light, cypress-wood and brick, single-story structure, designed on a streamlined "in-line" plan to accommodate a relatively casual and simplified lifestyle, and tucked into the right angle formed by the upper garden wall of the site, creating a sense of movement down the hillside on which the house sits.

# DEMOCRATIC HOMES

Wright had long believed, as he stated in the widely read *The Natural House*, which was published five years before his death, that "in integral architecture the room space itself must come through. We have no longer an outside and an inside as two separate things. Now the outside may come inside, and the inside may and does go outside. They are of each other." Direct contact with nature, to Wright, meant that people "actually derive countenance and sustenance from the 'atmosphere' of the things they live in or with. They are rooted in them just as a plant is in the soil."

The Willey House proved the first in a series of commissions for a rather different type of client from the wealthy business people with whom Wright had generally worked before 1929. The Usonian house, in its many variations, was developed, initially, at least, for a range of forward-thinking academics and journalists, with clear ideas about lifestyle, but also with limited budgets. It is characteristic of Wright's energy and enthusiasm that he rose so creatively to the challenge imposed by this financial stringency. In *An Autobiography* he outlines his approach to what he called "the moderate-cost house problem": "I am now certain that any approach to the new house … is fundamentally different. That house must be a pattern for more simplified and, at the same time, more gracious living; necessarily new, but suitable to living conditions as they might so well be in this country we live in today." He describes how he got rid of all unnecessary complications in construction, such as hips and valleys in the roofline, the basement, interior "trim," plastering, gutters, and downspouts. Instead of a garage, "a carport will do, with liberal overhead shelter, walls on two sides." In place of paint, a single coat of resinous oil on the wood; in place of radiators, gravity heat; in place of light fittings, "make the wiring system itself the light fixtures, light upon and down the room."

In terms of planning principles, the Usonian house is in a direct line of descent from the Prairie houses of Wright's earlier career. The treatment of the interior space as a single whole, broken into subspaces by carefully positioned vertical and horizontal masses, the long, low profile, and the general interpenetration of masses, appeared as early as 1902–3 in the Ward W. Willits House in Highland Park, Illinois. Crucial, too, to Wright's Usonian designs was the precise external orientation of the houses on their sites across the United States, so that each was integrated into the site and the rooms received sunlight at different times of day.

In terms of materials and construction, however, these houses reflect the clients' changed priorities. A simple construction-and-assembly process was devised to keep costs down and streamline the building process. As no complex masonry or carpentry skills were needed, it was possible for the Usonian houses to be built by local contractors (using Wright's own drawings) to a unit module and geometrical grid based on a standard plan, but customized to each site and homeowners' priorities. Indeed, so straightforward were the assembly methods that one prospective homeowner who had read about Wright and seen photographs of Taliesin, teacher Melvyn Maxwell Smith, set about learning construction techniques so that he could build a Usonian house for himself and his wife (1946, see pages 84–89) in Bloomfield Hills, Michigan, on an extremely modest budget.

Concrete, Wright's favored "gutter-rat" of materials, often formed the foundation of the houses, cast around heating pipes to do away with the necessity for conventional central heating, which Wright abhorred. "Gravity heating," as it is termed, the all-important open fire, good insulation, the arrangement of windows, and other factors enabled the houses to accommodate the vastly different climatic conditions that prevailed in the places where they were built, despite conforming to a simple, and to some degree standardized, plan.

The Hanna House (1935–37), Stanford, California (left), was Wright's first commission in the San Francisco region. Planned on a hexagonal module, the house seems to merge into the hillside on which it sits, with its floor and courtyard levels adjusting to the contours.

The living space in the first house built for Herbert Jacobs (1936, opposite) is both classic Wright, with its window wall, fluid living space, and use of natural materials, and classic Usonian, with its "L"-shaped floor plan, masonry core, and energy-efficient services. "A freedom of movement, a privacy too, is afforded by the general Usonian arrangement," wrote Wright in *An Autobiography*.

# RETHINKING FAMILY SPACES

Wright himself described the Herbert Jacobs House as the first Usonian house, calling it "Usonia 1." In *An Autobiography* he refutes those critics who dismissed the series of houses that followed as assembly-line repeats: "Let's see how far the Herbert Jacobs House … is a sensible house for the Jacobses. It wouldn't do for any but the Jacobses, of course." Jacobs was a newspaper reporter with a growing family. Simply designed on a grid of rectangular units, the house has an open, "L"-shaped floor plan. A central, masonry core contains the kitchen, utilities, and a great fireplace, focus of the living room and a familiar feature in Wright's work. In this case the masonry core also defines a small cellar, offering laundry space and boilers, the latter serving the energy-efficient, radiant central-heating system that circulates hot water through the 8-inch-thick (20-centimeter-thick) concrete floor slab. The living room is the largest space in the house, and is reached by a "hidden" entrance from the cantilevered carport roof; a window wall opens to the garden, and the dining area is connected to the living room along the main axis, with the bedrooms located in a separate wing beyond the kitchen.

The roof, which is carried mainly on the masonry walls, rises to a greater height over the living and dining areas and to a lower level over the bedroom and bathroom sections, where strips of clerestory windows at ceiling level ensure both light and privacy. The house "turns its back to the street," in Wright's phrase; the effect of the "L"-shaped plan is to make the house, which has a total area of under 1500 square feet (140 square meters), feel spacious, serene, and secure, also maximizing the effect of its orientation to the garden side.

The "brilliance of the Usonian house," according to the architecture critic Ada Louise Huxtable, is "the way in which it recognized the changes taking place in American society and domestic life." With the core of the house built around the kitchen space, or "workspace," as Wright termed it, with its essential flues and built-in units, this space became the hub of the house, around which the growing informality of family life might revolve. As Wright wrote in *The Natural House*, "The housewife herself thus planned for became the central figure in her ménage … She was now more hostess 'officio,' operating in gracious relation to her own home, instead of being a kitchen mechanic behind closed doors."

The Goetsch-Winckler House (1939, left), like many of the Usonian houses, was designed to a very specific brief, here for two academics. The living space flows seamlessly from the studio and library area at the far end, through the living area, with its focal fireplace, to a dining space, and beyond to the kitchen. The rows of clerestory windows and the warm timber complete the effect of simple comfort.

# VARIATIONS ON A THEME

Variants of the "L"-shaped Usonian house were developed in the form of "in-line" versions and, in some cases, nonstandard shapes. All, however, were flexible in that they could be adapted to any site, and with the capacity to be extended later for a growing, or more affluent, household by the addition of extra rooms on either end.

One of the most interesting and unusual variants is the hexagonal module that Wright used as the basis for the Paul R. and Jean Hanna House (1935–37), in Stanford, California, sometimes called the Honeycomb House due to the geometry of its plan. Again Wright's relationship with the client was a deciding factor. Paul and Jean Hanna were educators, who believed that human design could influence social behavior, and who, wishing to raise their family according to the progressive ideas of philosopher and educational reformer John Dewey, required a house that facilitated this aim. The hexagonal plan, with walls joined at 120-degree angles, was Wright's solution to this challenge. It creates a fluid, internal space with unrestricted sight lines; the kitchen workspace is centrally located, as in most Usonian houses, but here it is intrinsically linked not only with the living area, but with the playroom, so that Jean could observe and engage with her children as they played. The hexagon is used consistently throughout the design, from the ground plan and elevation on its spectacular, landscaped setting to its exterior and interior detail. As with the Jacobs House, the interior and exterior walls are of board-and-batten construction, thus eliminating the need for wall coverings. The timber used differed according to the site; in the Hanna House, it was redwood.

The house that Wright designed for Kathrine Winckler and Alma Goetsch in Okemos, Michigan, in 1939 is another variant, an "in-line" design in which the almost ritualistic living and dining spaces of the Prairie houses are no longer separate rooms, but open conveniently from the workspace area, which backs on to the essential Wrightian "sacred hearth." Goetsch and Winckler, both art teachers at Michigan State College (now Michigan State University), having seen the affordable Jacobs House in nearby Madison, wrote to Wright in October 1938 that they were "united in a common desire to have you build a house for us." They were quite specific in their requirements, both financial and practical: "we have a combined income of $4,500 a year and now pay $60.00 a month for the uncertain privilege of manipulating a few gadgets in a so-called four room apartment." Winckler particularly admired the fenestration of the Jacobs House's bedrooms: "All my life, I have resented the little holes in walls that people call windows and as I stood [there] I realized what it must mean to step out of bed and see earth and trees and sky all at once." Goetsch, on the other hand, as is clear from the joint specification of needs, had qualms about moving to the country and requested that Wright "make my bedroom give me a feeling of security."

The resulting design fulfilled the needs of both clients, providing an elegant, flexible central living space that doubled as a studio, with necessary social and study spaces for two academics without children. A single-line house, built on a 4-foot-square (1.22-meter-square) module, the concrete, redwood, and brick construction has a marked horizontal emphasis, enhanced by a continuous band of clerestory windows and topped by three levels of cantilevered roofs. As the land slopes away from the house, trees are visible through the high-level glazing, adding to its sense of harmonious serenity. The concrete-base foundation, which serves as the finished floor, is colored red and has the rectangular unit of the house scored into it.

Loren Pope, like Herbert Jacobs, was a journalist. He wrote to Wright with a request for a "Jacobs-style" house that would be affordable on a salary of $50 a week, stating: "There are certain things a man wants during life and of life. Material things and things of the spirit … one fervent wish … includes both. It is for a house created by you." Wright responded with enthusiasm, and the resulting design of 1939 is one of the simplest and most functionally effective expressions of the Usonian idea. An "L"-plan structure based on a 2 x 4-foot (61 x 122-centimeter) rectangular grid, it is a typical cypress-batten, dry-wall construction around a brick core, with a flat roof, cantilevered carport, heated concrete floor slab, and a uniform treatment of exterior and interior walls—and it cost just $7000. A distinctive feature of the house is its extensive use of true bald cypress, cut into complex fretwork panels to provide light from above in the living area, which was lit from both sides by a variation on the Wrightian "light screen" of floor-to-ceiling windows. Originally raised at Falls Church, Virginia, the construction was so flexible that it was moved in its entirety by its second owner, Mrs. Marjorie Leighey, to its present site in Alexandria, Virginia, when threatened by the construction of an interstate highway in 1964.

Viewed from this interior angle (opposite), the relation of the Goetsch–Winckler House to its setting is visible through the windows; merging with its woodland site, it seems to float in the trees.

Another commission designed on a tight budget, the Pope–Leighey House (above and left, detail) also takes an "L"-shaped form and is noteworthy for its use of fretwork cypress panels, which admit additional light.

# USONIA RECOGNIZED

In January 1938 the Jacobs House was featured among recent projects by the seventy-year-old Wright, including Fallingwater and the S.C. Johnson & Son Co. Administration Building (1936), Racine, Wisconsin, in a long, illustrated article in *Time* magazine, with Wright being granted the ultimate accolade of his portrait on the cover, alongside the headline, "Frank Lloyd Wright, Usonian Architect." Subsequent lecture tours, publications, and television appearances did much to bring Wright's work in this, his fully mature period of creativity, to public attention. The result was an enhanced reputation and new clients for this innovative form of house that was adapted to their needs and anticipated a new lifestyle for changing times. A further high point was the exhibition of Wright's work at New York's Museum of Modern Art in 1940, which he called "the

show to end all shows," the same year in which he established the Frank Lloyd Wright Foundation. It was initially intended to construct a full-sized Usonian house in the museum's sculpture garden as part of the exhibit, but, as scholar Kathryn Smith has documented, opposition from John D. Rockefeller, Jr., led to the cancellation of this plan.

Wright also lectured on international platforms. A few months before the outbreak of World War II, in one of a series of lectures to the Royal Institute of British Architects in London, England, that was later published under the title *An Organic Architecture: The Architecture of Democracy*, Wright explained: "I think Usonian is an excellent name, having its roots in union, as we have our national life in it." Using slides of both the Jacobs House and the hexagonal Hanna House as examples, he elaborated further on the term as "expressing the inner spirit of our democracy, which by and large is not yet so very democratic after all, as you may know."

After the war, Usonians often followed on as new versions of the original houses, as with the Melvyn Maxwell Smith House of 1946, a quintessentially Usonian house with an "L"-shaped plan. The Smiths had originally approached Wright at Taliesin West in 1941. Using red tidewater cypress throughout, in its use of fretwork screens and window detailing, the Smith House is reminiscent of the prewar Loren Pope House.

An interview with Mrs. Sarah Smith, published in the *Journal of Architectural Education* in 1986, gives a clear sense of the close and cooperative working relationship that Wright established with his clients: "We knew he knew just exactly what type of a home to design for us. What a beautiful interview! I will never forget it." Wright was also prepared to be both flexible with, and supportive of, his clients. When "Smithy," as Sarah called her husband, received the plans and got quotes, he was daunted by the price and told Wright that he could not afford to build the house. It was Wright who suggested that he organize the project himself: "Smith, you can build this house. You go home and study those plans … You can contract that house yourself." So "Smithy" studied the plans closely and found that he wanted to make a few changes to them. He consulted Wright about these, saying that if Wright disapproved, he would, of course, drop the idea. Wright looked at the changes, tapping his pencil, as described by Mrs. Smith, and then told her that her husband would make a fine architect: "And Smithy said right then and there, he felt he received his degree in architecture."

"A modest house is this Usonian house. A dwelling place that has no feeling at all for 'the grand' except as the house extends itself in the flat parallel to the ground, a companion to the horizon," wrote Wright in *An Autobiography*. The Melvyn Maxwell Smith House (above and opposite) is another classic Usonian design, making extensive use of the fretwork panels also seen at the Pope–Leighey House (above, left). Here they function both as the principal decorative motif and as a fully developed "light screen." The natural timber that Wright used—cypress in this case—was more labor-saving and economical than paintwork, requiring no more than a single coat of preservative.

The dining space in the Melvyn Maxwell Smith House (pictured on page 86) was more clearly delineated as a separate space than in most Usonian houses, at the Smiths' request: they liked to entertain and wanted a dedicated area.

A

B

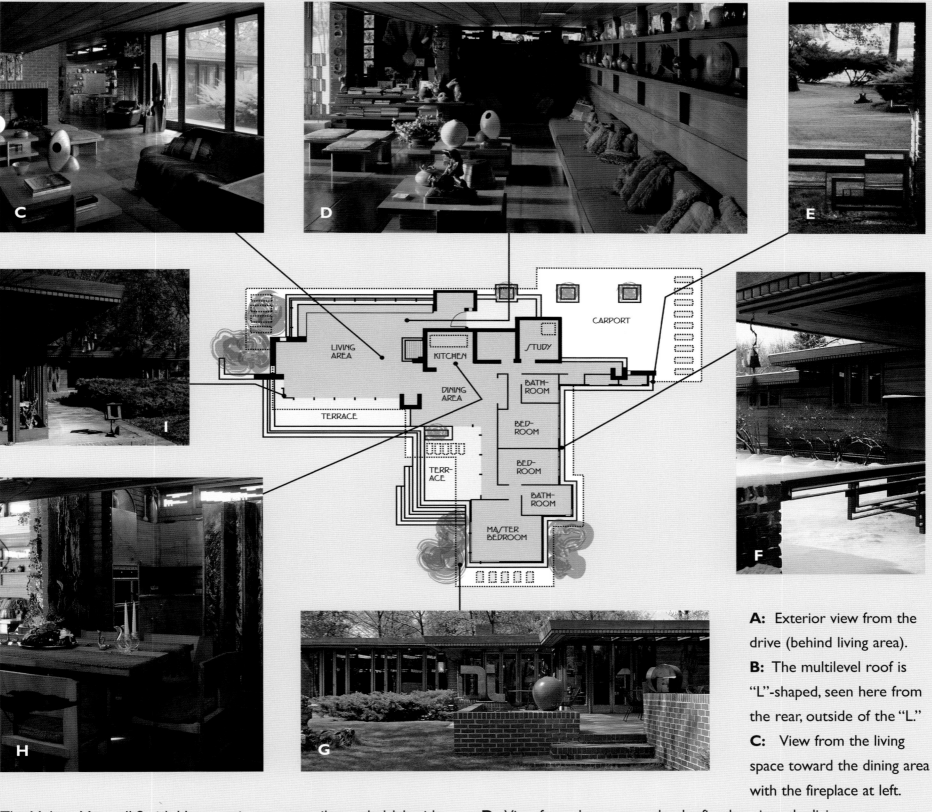

C

D

E

I

LIVING
AREA

KITCHEN

STUDY

CARPORT

DINING
AREA

BATH-
ROOM

TERRACE

BED-
ROOM

TERR-
ACE

BED-
ROOM

BATH-
ROOM

MASTER
BEDROOM

F

H

G

The Melvyn Maxwell Smith House enjoys a tranquil, wooded, lakeside setting on a 3-acre (1.2-hectare) property and is oriented so that the terraces and glazed walls, on the inside of the "L" shape, overlook the lake. The living-room photograph (following pages) reveals that the living space is open, yet secluded. The masonry core and pillars carry the cantilevered roof, while the walls, of sandwiched cypress, are not load-bearing. This is among Wright's last such homes, the later ones having masonry walls, as William Allin Storrer has noted.

**A:** Exterior view from the drive (behind living area).

**B:** The multilevel roof is "L"-shaped, seen here from the rear, outside of the "L."

**C:** View from the living space toward the dining area with the fireplace at left.

**D:** View from the entrance, by the fireplace, into the living space.

**E:** Metalwork details of gate and spiral motif, finished in Cherokee red.

**F:** The bedroom wing, viewed from the carport.

**G:** The open, glazed aspect of the house—the inside of the "L" shape—and bedroom-wing terraces, with wall (for privacy) in the foreground.

**H:** The kitchen/workspace, located within the house's central masonry core, viewed from the dining area.

**I:** View from outside the living area toward the bedroom wing.

The Hagan House (also known as Kentuck Knob, 1954, these pages), in Chalkhill, Pennsylvania, appears to grow organically out of the hillside on which it is situated. One end takes the form of a ship's prow, echoing the great triangular terrace at Taliesin West, and anticipating

the similar prowlike space that forms an integral part of Wright's plan for the Marin County Civic Center (pages 168–71). The plan is based on hexagonal modules. The main construction materials are local sandstone, quarried on site, and tidewater red cypress.

Isadore J. Zimmerman and his wife sought Wright's help after reading his *An Autobiography*; new potential clients of Wright often approached him directly with requests for particular needs. In the resulting Isadore J. Zimmerman House (1950), in Manchester, New Hampshire, the living area was designed to double as a performance space for the Zimmermans and their musical friends, and Wright also designed a quartet music stand as part of the furniture. In order to ensure privacy on the street side of the house, Wright designed "keyhole" windows placed high on the brick base of the building, in contrast to the floor-to-ceiling, glazed areas on the terrace side of the "in-line" plan. The choice of upland Georgia cypress and red-glazed brick, terra-cotta tile for the roof, and red-toned Colundrum, a newly patented sealant, for the concrete floors gives the Zimmerman House a particular warmth and elegance. Wright called this house a "classic Usonian," and the Zimmermans hailed it delightedly as "the most beautiful home in the world."

The living area in the Zimmerman House (below), in Manchester, New Hampshire, was designed to serve also as a performance space for the Zimmermans' musical evenings, but the great hearth still strikes a dominant note. The contrast between the high, narrow band of windows on the street side, permitting light into the house, but guarding the residents' privacy, and the translucent window-wall on the garden side is strikingly clear in this photograph.

Don Schaberg, who commissioned this house in Okemos, Michigan (1950, above and right), stated that more than 55,000 bricks were used in its construction, both inside and outside, and certainly the views here are dominated by the mellow brickwork. Planned as an "L" shape, it has a central kitchen and dining section, with bedrooms to the southwest and the living area to the northeast, adjoining a carport, another of Wright's major innovations.

While the Usonian houses share many characteristics, including ground plans and various cost- and energy-efficient features, each one is also an individual response to the particular site and to the client's requirements. The single-story William Palmer House (above, left, and overleaf) conforms to the ridge of its hilly site. The brick that forms the basic construction material, known as "Cranbrook brick" because it was used in Eliel Saarinen's nearby Cranbrook Academy, was made by ClayCraft of Columbus, Ohio, which also made the matching pierced blocks. Glazed bands of the decorative blocks bring light into the house, recalling the textile-block houses and the fretwork panels in a number of other Usonian houses.

In 1950, too, William Palmer and his wife, Mary, commissioned an intriguing variant on the "in-line" Usonian for a hillside site in Ann Arbor, Michigan. The design is based on an equilateral triangle, the dramatic exterior being enhanced by the extraordinary projection of the prowlike roof sheltering the terrace. The use of brick throughout is noteworthy for its coloration and consistency: both the sand-mold brick and the block that formed the house came from the same source and were fired in the same fashion. A grid of parallelograms scored in the red-sealed floor underlines the subtle geometry, and the warm tones of the house are carried through in the red tidewater-cypress boards of the ceiling.

In the Usonian houses, Wright kept hallways compact in order to save space and to heighten the sense of openness when moving from a confined to an expansive interior space. Wright used this technique, "compression and release," as seen on these pages in the William Palmer House, in many buildings throughout his career. He sometimes designed hallways that turned through angles, for increased impact on approaching the living space.

# USONIAN AUTOMATICS

In his final response to a changing world, Wright adapted his textile-block system of the 1920s in order to simplify construction for home-builders. In these "Usonian automatics," as Wright termed them in *The Natural House*, "we have eliminated the need for skilled labor by prefabricating all plumbing, heating and wiring, so each appurtenance system may come into the building in a factory made package, easily installed by making several simple connections provided during block-construction."

The Eric Brown House, in Kalamazoo, Michigan, of 1949 was designed to be part of a larger cooperative community scheme, Parkwyn Village, overlooking a lake, but only four houses were built. The Brown House was constructed from textile blocks, with mahogany trim, on a square module. Some of the blocks were pierced and glazed to give privacy on the street side, while in the living room, window walls opened on to views of the lake.

Wright was working on the Usonian automatics at the time of his death. In *The Future of Architecture*, he wrote, "What is needed most in architecture today is the very thing that is most needed in life—integrity. ... The Usonian House, then, aims to be … integral to site, integral to environment, integral to the life of the inhabitants."

The Gerald Tonkens House (1954, living room pictured above), in Amberley Village, Cincinnati, Ohio, is hailed by William Allin Storrer in *The Architecture of Frank Lloyd Wright* as "a major statement in the history of Usonian automatic houses." A clerestory of pierced blocks lights the work space, and a stacked double series of blocks illuminates the living area. Wright's grandson, Eric Wright, helped to supervise construction.

In the Turkel House (1955, left), in Detroit, Michigan, the whole exterior façade is articulated by the pierced, light-admitting concrete blocks that serve instead of windows. The living area and hearth of the Eric Brown House (1949, opposite), in Parkwyn Village, Kalamazoo, Michigan, are seen here from the corner opposite the dining area.

# "A LOOK OVER THE RIM OF THE WORLD"

◧ ◧ ◧

# Taliesin West

◧ ◧ ◧

"Just imagine what it would be like on top of the world looking over the universe at sunrise or at sunset with clear sky in between. Light and air bathing all the worlds of creation in all the color there ever was—all the shapes and outlines ever devised … all beyond the reach of the finite mind. Well, that was our place on the mesa and our buildings had to fit in. It was a new world to us … [with] … an esthetic, even ascetic, idealization of space, of breadth and height and of strange firm forms … [For] our buildings certain forms abounded. There were simple characteristic silhouettes to go by, tremendous drifts and heaps of sunburned desert rocks were nearby to be used. We got it all together with the landscape—where God is all and man is nought."

—*An Autobiography*

*A view outside Wright's office (left), with sculptural boulders, and foreground detail of the colorful walls of rubblestone. "Magnificent! Beyond words to describe!" enthused Wright over his desert "paradise"; the plans were "inspired by the character and beauty of that wonderful site," as seen more fully in the photograph overleaf.*

# THE "PROMISED LAND"

Frank Lloyd Wright's desert encampment in Arizona, finally named Taliesin West after earlier suggested names failed to appeal, is one of his most personal projects, like the original Taliesin. And, like the original Taliesin, it was both home and workspace for the Taliesin Fellowship, remaining in a permanent state of adaptation and development as it changed with the life and work of its creator.

Wright had first gotten to know the Arizona desert in 1927, when he was involved in the design for the Arizona Biltmore Hotel in Phoenix and was taken to see the site for a desert resort proposed by local landowner Dr. Alexander Chandler. Wright was enchanted, writing in his *An Autobiography*, "Well, there could be nothing more inspiring to an architect on this earth than that spot of Arizona desert he took me out to see." Wright and his team decided to camp in the desert while they worked on the project, and constructed their own temporary accommodation, which Wright called "Ocatilla," after the ocotillo plant found there.

The idea of transferring the whole Taliesin community, then numbering about thirty people, from Wisconsin to Arizona on a regular basis for the winter months first arose during the early 1930s, in response to concerns about Wright's health and about the cost of maintaining and heating the extended Taliesin. In fall 1934 Wright contacted Chandler requesting a temporary base while he looked for a site where he could establish a winter camp. In the event the search for a site took three years, a period that Wright later described as a pilgrimage to the Promised Land: "By this time that vast desert region, Silence and Beauty, was as familiar to us as our part of Wisconsin. ... Finally I learned of a site twenty-six miles from Phoenix and across the desert of vast Paradise Valley. On up to a great mesa in the mountains. On the mesa just below McDowell Peak we stopped, turned and looked around. The top of the world ..."

Wright initially acquired 600 acres (2,428,200 square meters) of dry and rugged land, dramatically situated at the foot of the McDowell Mountains, with an extensive view over the landscape and a commanding backdrop, and began, with his apprentice team from Taliesin, to plan his "winter camp." He had already laid down the principles in his initial response to the desert: "Arizona character seems to cry out for a space-loving architecture of its own. The straight line and flat plane, sun-lit, must come here—of all places—but they should become the dotted line, the broad, low, extended plane textured because in all this astounding desert there is not one hard undotted line to be seen ... a pattern of what appropriate Arizona architecture might well be lies there hidden in these mesas ..."

A further inspiration was the evidence of prehistoric Hohokam (Native American) occupation of the site. Wright and his team uncovered potsherds and grinding stones as they cleared the ground, and a large group of boulders was found to be incised with ancient carvings. The site appears to have been a ceremonial gathering point, a numinous "high place," and in his final plan for it, Wright aligned the central, open space with the area where the major Hohokam finds had been discovered, while his wife, Olgivanna, described the process of construction as "not ... building but excavating."

Certain of the great boulders that were found on the site, distinguished either by size or by their incised carving, were incorporated by Wright as part of the plan from the outset. These included one at the beginning of the pergola, just opposite Wright's office, and one on the main terrace, in front of the drafting room. As Neil Levine demonstrates in *The Architecture of Frank Lloyd Wright* (1996), they formed the culmination of a processional approach, which spiraled away from the main boulevard running across the valley floor and approached Taliesin West in a series of sweeps and arcs, offering a continu-

ally changing vista of the camp set against its mountain backdrop. The spiraling pattern continued inside the camp as the main axis rotated in a series of carefully designed angles, each marked by a great boulder. Wright's office dominated the entrance court, and the boulder that he placed outside it served as a pivot, marking the point at which the axis swung through 45 degrees. Here the boulder was incised with the characteristic Hohokam double-square interlocking spiral, for Wright a powerful symbol of the site as a cultural continuum.

"Taliesin in the Desert," an early name for the complex, seen here (above) in Wright's perspective drawing in pencil and colored pencil.

"On the desert slopes at Taliesin West there is always a breeze," Wright wrote. Pools and fountains help to cool the gardens (below).

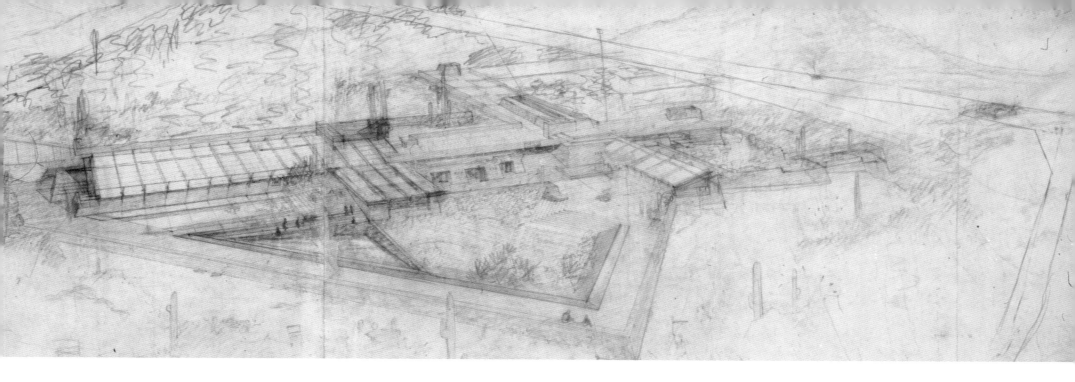

The plan was based on a west-southwest orientation, with a pergola forming its spine, and consisted of five basic units—workshops, Wright's office, drafting room, living quarters for the Wright family, and quarters for the rest of the Fellowship, the apprentices. At its heart was the open, central space, the loggia, around which were grouped the kitchen and dining room, and which formed the link between the drafting room and the "L"-shaped main house. In this sense Taliesin West was the opposite of its predecessor in Wisconsin. As Wright himself wrote: "It was a new world to us and cleared the slate of the pastoral loveliness of our place in Southern Wisconsin. Instead came an esthetic, even ascetic, idealization of space, of breadth and height and of strange firm forms, a sweep that was a spiritual cathartic for Time if indeed Time continued to exist."

# EXTENDING "OCATILLA"

Taliesin was formed as a ring of living, working, and service facilities set around a central complex of courts, gardens, and terraces, with its inhabitants working together, but living separately. At Taliesin West, however, the center of the diagonal plan was devoted to the drafting room, with a great, triangular terrace forming a prow overlooking the desert and unifying the main communal elements. While some apprentices continued to live in tents and other temporary structures, Taliesin West was conceived as a planned community in a manner less developed in Wright's thinking when he built the original Taliesin. In this sense Taliesin West has a connection with the spirit of decentralization, self-sufficiency, and reverence for the land that inspired such projects as Wright's unrealized Broadacre City scheme, which Wright conceived in Wisconsin and continued to promote for the rest of his life.

In the gardens of
Taliesin West, sculptures take their place
beside boulders and cacti native to the Sonoran Desert (above).

In terms of its three-dimensional appearance, Taliesin West is less clearly differentiated from Wright's other work. Taking the form of a low-lying, essentially one-story, complex of distinct units linked by a terrace, walkways, and bridges, it has echoes of both earlier and later schemes. The basic material was the local rock, as Wright described: "For the design of our buildings certain forms already abounded. There were simple characteristic silhouettes to go by, tremendous drifts and heaps of sunburned desert rocks were nearby to be used. We got it all together with the landscape—where God is all and man is naught—as a more permanent extension of 'Ocatilla,' the first canvas-topped desert camp in the world of Architecture. By youthful enthusiasm posterity was to ponder the real thing."

Taliesin fellows at work, bathed in the filtered light of the drafting room (left), which remains in use today. The windows at far left are also seen in the exterior view (below), taken from beside the pool, looking across the stairs and terrace. The seamless blend of indoor and outdoor space, in and beyond the garden room (overleaf).

The massive walls of the complex were constructed of the richly colored desert stone, set into wooden forms and then concreted, so that they appeared to form a monumental mosaic that reflected the intense colors of the desert mountains. The walls were designed to slope inward at an angle of 15 degrees, echoing in a third dimension the angles of the plan, and giving the impression that the structure grew naturally out of the surrounding desert. "That desert camp belonged to the desert as though it had stood there for centuries," Wright reflected in *An Autobiography*.

The original roof covering was of a much more transient nature, consisting as it did of canvas panels stretched across an exposed framework of rough-sawn, redwood trusses. This diffused the harsh desert sun, and ingeniously designed panels could be opened to the least breeze. Wright described lyrically how: "On a fair day when these white tops and side flaps were flung open the desert air and the birds flew clear through."

The internal spaces created by this combination of masonry walls and floating roof took differing forms. The two largest communal rooms—the 100-foot-long (39-meter-long) drafting room and the 56-foot-long (17-meter-long) garden room in the Wrights' living quarters, which served as the social center—consisted of a canopy-style shelter of wood-and-canvas frames placed over widely spaced masonry supports. The drafting room was originally open both to the pergola to the north and the terrace to the south, while the garden room opened on to terraces and gardens, and the effect of both was to give a sense of shelter, but not enclosure; they were as much outdoor as indoor spaces. Other internal areas were designed to be much more focused and enclosed. Wright's office was set into a graded slope and thus partly underground, with roof-level windows opening out on to the rise, while the movie theater was a small, rectangular, solid masonry structure with air vents only, and no windows.

A crucial feature, especially in this arid landscape, and one that Wright used throughout the site, was the water that, contrary to local wisdom, he and his team found when they sank a 500-foot-deep (152-meter-deep) well. The gardens and terraces were both cooled and enlivened by water features that became an integral feature of the plan. One of the gardens, Wright wrote, was a "great prow running out into the mesa overlooking the world, wide desert below, a triangular pool nestling in it," and "another garden sequestered for quiet, another plunge-pool, water raining down from the wall around it."

Sunlight and shade, curves and angles, contrasting textures, and a desert palette of reds, pinks, and umbers combine to give Taliesin West its singular, poetic quality, as these exterior details illustrate. The pergola (above) extends alongside the drafting room; a rank of trusses (below); a sculptural, square-spiral sign mounted on the lighting tower (opposite).

So organically at one with its setting is Taliesin West that Wright's wife Olgivanna once observed that it seemed more excavated than built; or, as Ada Louise Huxtable noted in her biography of the architect, "as the camp rose from the desert, it disappeared into it." These images of the kitchen bell tower (opposite); the lighting tower that supports the square-spiral sign (right); and the boulder at the entrance, which was found on the site and bears ancient markings (below, right), illustrate how art is inspired by both landscape and the objects and symbols of the prehistoric peoples who inhabited it, so that the natural and man-made are unified and informed by each other's inherent beauty. Bruce Brooks Pfeiffer, a former apprentice, has led the tremendous task of preserving Wright's legacy by archiving his drawings, plans, and writings at the Frank Lloyd Wright Archives at Taliesin West. He wrote of both Taliesins that they "seemed to live and breathe alongside [Wright], combining the magnificent idiosyncrasies of his complex nature and personal genius."

Modifications to the original plan were made almost immediately as Wright returned to his winter retreat each year with fresh eyes. Some were practical responses to the need for additional space as his practice expanded during the late 1940s and 1950s, and as the original materials showed signs of wear and tear. An early and significant change was the addition of a second-story deck over the loggia and dining space to accommodate visitors. The canvas roofs were rearranged, renewed, and eventually replaced by more durable synthetic materials, principally fiberglass and steel, which still retained the translucent effect of the originals. From about 1945 glass, which had not featured in the early plans, was increasingly used.

More interesting, in terms of understanding Wright's own priorities, as Neil Levine has shown, is the sequence of changes that he made along the axis of the complex in order to frame the mountain peak rising in the distance. In the earliest plan, the spinelike pergola was the main feature that emphasized the relationship between the camp and its setting. In the late 1940s, a stone bridge was built farther east along the same axis to link the rear of the Wrights' living quarters with the movie theater. This straddled an elongated pool and was carried on two inclined piers that echoed the distant mountain slope, while a tall water tower signposted the viewing point. In the 1950s Wright added a rough pediment to the bridge immediately above the pool and continuing the line of the two piers. The effect was to transform the whole into a monumental gateway that appeared to invite the distant mountain into the communal space.

Wright's own passion for, and engagement with, Taliesin West remained unwavering until his death. "Superlatives are exhausting and usually a bore," he observed, "but we lived, moved, and had our being in superlatives for years. And we were never bored."

# THE "MOTHER ART"

❑ ❑ ❑

## Mature Expressions of Organic Architecture

❑ ❑ ❑

"True architecture ... is poetry. A good building is the greatest of poems when it is organic architecture. The fact that the building faces and is reality and serves while it releases life, makes daily life better worth living and makes all the necessities happier because of useful living in it, makes the building none the less poetry, but more truly so. Every great architect is—necessarily—a great poet."

—*An Organic Architecture*, 1939
(in *Collected Writings*, Vol. 3)

*Fallingwater (left), one of Wright's most successful and iconic creations, has been described by Bruce Brooks Pfeiffer as "perhaps the greatest blend of building and environment ever achieved in domestic architecture."*

Bear Run, the site of Fallingwater (opposite and right), had been acquired in 1916 by Edgar J. Kaufmann's family business, Pittsburgh's largest department store. By 1934 the family wanted to replace their modest summer camp with something more substantial. When Kaufmann first took Wright to the site of the waterfall where the family loved to fish and swim, he assumed that Wright would choose the flatter, wider, south bank, but in the event Wright placed the house on the steep north bank, projecting out over the waterfall itself.

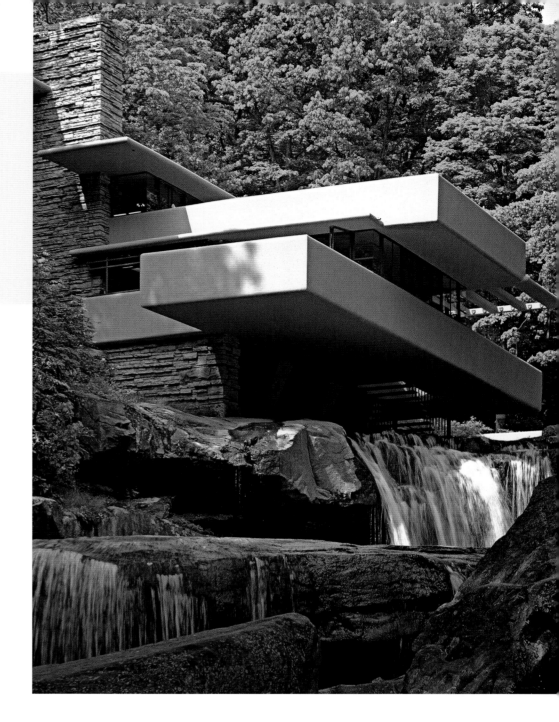

The designs that Frank Lloyd Wright produced during the last two decades of his life increasingly revealed his preoccupation with reconciling the "Mother Art," as he deemed architecture, with Mother Nature. While elements of this philosophy of "organic architecture" are expressed in even the early designs, such as the Winslow House (1893–94), and, indeed, Wright himself defined organic architecture rather differently over time, his later work shows an ever-increasing confidence and ambition. His 1935 plans for Broadacre City, a decentralized, land-based community that never reached fruition, demonstrate his concern to offer an agrarian alternative to Le Corbusier's revolutionary plans for a modern technological city, as well as his ability to reconcile the practical and spiritual needs of the individual with respect for the natural world, and his willingness to use modern materials and building methods while retaining a craftsman's eye for detail and tradition.

By the mid-1930s, after a period of both personal and professional hardship, Wright's career was beginning to flourish again. The establishment of the Taliesin Fellowship brought him the assistance and energy of the loyal and admiring apprentices, and in his third wife, Olgivanna, he found a true partner who shared and stimulated his thinking and gave him both practical and emotional support. By 1938 he was sufficiently acclaimed that the January issue of *Architectural Forum* was devoted to his work, which prompted him to discuss his ideas about organic architecture ("It is a sense of the whole that is lacking in the 'modern' building I have seen"), and to identify certain "expressions of principle." These include the sense of ground—topography, organic features, the idea of growth; the sense of shelter, particularly relevant to his domestic commissions; the sense of materials, always a fundamental concern for Wright; the sense of space, and the grouping of utilitarian features so that space could be either magnified or interrupted; the importance of order and proportion; and technique, the "ways and means." His work of the 1930s brilliantly combines his high-soaring ideas of place and space with the painstaking and exact engineering required to realize them, and paved the way for the still more pioneering, ingenious work of his final decade.

# IN/PIRED BY IT/ /ITE

Fallingwater (1935–37), the house commissioned by Edgar J. Kaufmann, Sr., at Bear Run, Pennsylvania, dates from the same period as Broadacre City and illustrates the same concerns and characteristics. It is also a place of quite extraordinary beauty and drama, a structure that is intimately connected with its natural setting, yet whose ordered, geometric lines are uncompromisingly modern. It was one of Wright's most congenial and positive commissions; writing in the January 1938 issue of *Architectural Forum*, he described the contributing elements: "The inspiration of a site, the cooperation of an intelligent, appreciative client."

The Kaufmann family, owners of a thriving Pittsburgh department store, had used the site as a rustic weekend retreat for years before Edgar J. Kaufmann, Sr., whose son joined the Taliesin Fellowship in 1934, invited Wright to visit "the waterfall in the woods" and commissioned him to design a country house here. Today considered the high point of Wright's domestic architecture, and perhaps the most famous private house in

Fallingwater's vertical stone shafts, built of stone that was quarried nearby, are broken up by a series of horizontal concrete balconies that project from the rock ledge, overhanging the stream (above).

Wright's detailed perspective drawing of Fallingwater from the southeast side, just downstream (overleaf), shows two figures looking from their respective balcony vantage points at the waterfall below.

history, Fallingwater realizes Wright's lifelong ideal of a living place entirely at one with its setting, the setting in this case being a wooded glen in the western Pennsylvanian highlands threaded through by a stream and the waterfall that gave the house its name, whose falling water could be heard throughout the house. In *Architectural Forum*, Wright described his commission, its setting, and his vision thus: "this extension of the cliff beside a mountain stream, making living space over and above the stream upon several terraces upon which a man who loved the place sincerely, one who liked to listen to the waterfall, might well live."

A series of soaring, smooth, cantilevered balconies anchored in solid rock and woven together by roughly textured native sandstone walls laid up in alternating courses, Fallingwater is constructed on three levels, with cantilevered terraces of reinforced concrete extending far out in four directions. Their mellow, buff-colored planes contrast effectively with the vertical shafts of mitered glass, sandstone, and steel that crown the composition. Canopy slabs protect terraces and balconies from the elements and enhance the filtered light that illuminates the glen, also providing, as Wright explained, "the softened diffused lighting for which the indweller is invariably grateful, I have found."

The southern façade, with its glazed walls below illuminating the living room and smaller terraces at the sides, and with its great terrace above, overlooks the stream, and the various seating areas are grouped to take full advantage of the views on all sides. The lowest of the great cantilevered balconies forms the main floor of the house, and holds a single, stone-flagged, open living room, which serves as combined dining and sitting space, reception, and library. The living space is continuous from inside to outside; where one balcony overlaps another, plate-glass doors and windows mark the passage between interior and terrace. This main floor rises from the rock ledges that anchor the house, which are reprised in the rough walls and load-bearing piers of native sandstone. A shallow, open, "floating" stairway descends from here to water level, to a plunge pool just above the falls. Above the main floor, another balcony holds a terrace forming the roof of the living room, together with several bedrooms, each with its own terrace.

Much of the informal furniture that Wright designed for the living room was built into the room's structure, including the long, padded bench below the windows. Freestanding walnut furniture was made to order in Milwaukee by Gillen Woodworking Company, supervised by Taliesin apprentice Edgar Tafel, and North Carolina walnut and walnut veneer appear throughout the house. Natural boulders found on the site were incorporated into the design of the hearth, further amalgamating Mother Nature and the "Mother Art."

The house's three bedrooms, kitchen, and utility areas comprised only a small proportion of the floor space, and in 1939 a guest house, with garage and servants' quarters, was added on a slope above the main house. It was accessed by means of a winding, covered walkway made up of curved and geometric, concrete forms. Similar forms encircle some of the trees in the garden—visual ribbons that link the complex and its setting.

Wright's floor plan for Fallingwater fits neatly over the triangular rock ledge on which the house sits; his first designs for the house were drawn at an angle to conform to the topography on his site plan. The great terraces cantilevered out from the stone structural supports run parallel with the course of the stream, and also give the house the southeastern orientation that Wright favored. The effect, as Neil Levine shows, is that the whole house, in aligning with the stream, seems to pivot with the landscape and to absorb within itself the movement and flow of the water.

**A:** A view of the living area, with its diffused light. The materials, tones, and textures are in harmony with the natural world outside.

**B:** For the floor, Wright used flagstones that resemble the stones found in the bed of the stream. They are waxed to reflect the changing light.

**C:** An ice-bound view of the rock ledge that supports the bars of the trellis over the drive.

**D:** Fallingwater's plunge pool, stairs up to the living area, and two side terraces above.

**E:** The view across the living area to a side terrace (doors seen at right) and the glass enclosure (left) that opens to the stairs leading down to the plunge pool. The stairs and terrace are seen in photograph D.

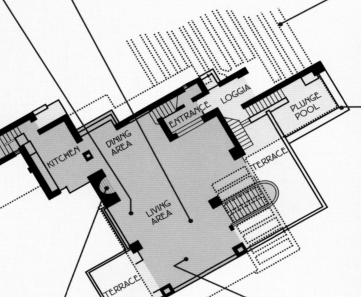

**F:** The layering effect of the cantilevered balconies of the house echoes the naturally occurring layers of the rock ledge.

**G:** In front of the fireplace, Wright incorporated a boulder that is part of the rock ledge; it protrudes through the flagged floor.

**H:** The house appears to float above the falling water, as though its surfaces are part of the rock through which the stream falls.

# "REMARKABLY SUCCESSFUL"

Curves and geometric forms also featured prominently in the S.C. Johnson & Son Co. Administration Building, or Johnson Wax Building, in Racine, Wisconsin, that Wright designed in 1936. Commissioned by Herbert F. Johnson, this extraordinary building came in hugely over budget, even by Wright's standards, but was—and is—hailed as such a landmark of corporate architecture that the Johnson family no doubt considered this money well spent, not least if, as a result of Wright's stated aim to make it "as inspiring a place to work in as any cathedral was in which to worship," inspired workers equaled increased productivity.

And in describing the administration complex in his *An Autobiography*, Wright hinted at its importance: "To enumerate in detail or even catalogue the innovations to be found in this one building would require more time and patient attention on your part, and mine too, than either of us cares to give it. So let's say here that it is technically, and in the entire realm of the scientific art of Architecture, one of the world's remarkably successful structures." Indeed, as well as boasting a radical, handsome design (there were no internal walls, but simply a large, open-plan hall with a mezzanine—an arrangement that may seem familiar enough in commercial buildings today, but was quite revolutionary at the time), the steel-reinforced

In *An Autobiography* Wright described the Johnson Wax Building (above, the photograph also shows the later S.C. Johnson & Son Co. Research Tower at left; and opposite): "This building by way of a natural use of steel in tension, appears to lift and float in light and air; 'miraculously light dendriforms' standing up against the sky take on an integral character as plastic units of a plastic building construction, *emphasizing* space instead of standing up in the way as mere inserts for support-destroying space."

The Great Workroom (above), designed to accommodate the main clerical workforce, was air-conditioned, with top lighting, and further daylight entering through horizontal "cornices" of Pyrex tubing set at several levels. Jonathan Lipman, in *Frank Lloyd Wright and the Johnson Wax Buildings* (1986), describes this as "so rich that it appeared to have substance, the light seemed to be the matter of which the great room was made."

Throughout the Johnson Wax complex are spaces with curving forms, soft colors, and filtered light from the Pyrex tubing, as seen in the advertising department's reception area (right).

building incorporated the latest technology. Fireproof, air-conditioned, heated with a system of underfloor panels—referred to as "gravity heating"—soundproofed, earthquake-proof, it was also fully fitted out and furnished to an exacting specification. Wright designed handsome, contoured office furniture especially for the building, including steel-and-wood desks and chairs that harmonized with the restful, terra-cotta color of the file cabinets. No ordinary office complex, then, it even included leisure facilities like a squash court and movie theater. "It was meant," according to the architect, "to be a socio-architectural interpretation of modern business at its top and best."

Wright may have referred to the "scientific art of Architecture" in his summing-up of the Johnson Wax Building's merits, but there are nevertheless clear allusions to Mother Nature in this corporate structure, not least in the cream-colored, reinforced-concrete columns of the Great Workroom—the building's centerpiece—which have been described as resembling lily pads, mushrooms, or trees. Indeed, the Great Workroom's most notable—and at the time, radical—feature of construction was, as Wright wrote in *An Autobiography*, the "simple repetition of slender, hollow monolithic dendriform shafts or stems—the stems standing tip-toe in small brass shoes bedded at the floor level." These dendriform (treelike) columns, each supporting

either the roof or the mezzanine level, appear to be a living forest within the great central room, forming integral elements of a spatially continuous whole and, as Wright described in *An Autobiography*, "emphasizing space instead of standing up in the way as mere inserts for support."

Another remarkable feature of the Johnson Wax Building is the Pyrex-glass tubing that replaces plate-glass windows and, in the form of cleverly placed glass "cornices" (continuous, horizontal bands of tubing) and skylights, illuminates its workspaces, atria, and walkways with soft, natural light. Wright avoided the use of windows with which to break up the Cherokee-red-brick walls because the industrial surroundings of the site could not provide

attractive views, yet there is no lack of natural light entering the uncluttered interior. In the Great Workroom, for instance, diffused light floods through the skylighted gaps between the ceiling-height "lily pads" at the top of the supportive columns. The experimental tubular glazing did suffer from leaks and other problems, but later modifications would resolve them.

In 1943 Wright was called upon to build a multistory research, or laboratory, tower for the expanding company. The resulting S.C. Johnson & Son Co. Research Tower was executed in alternating bands of the same Cherokee red brick and glass tubing, so that it constituted a harmonious addition to the complex.

# SPREADING ITS WINGS

In 1937, while Wright was still working on the S.C. Johnson & Son Co. Administration Building in Racine, Wisconsin, Herbert F. Johnson (whom he knew as "Hib") charged him with designing a country house nearby for himself, his second wife, and four children. As Wright later recalled, in his revised *An Autobiography*: "This is probably one of the most complete, best constructed and most expensive houses it has ever been my good fortune to build."

The house was called "Wingspread" "because spread its wings it would." The "spread-wings" effect that is such a notable feature of the predominantly red-brick and timber Wingspread House, which Wright later described as the "last of the prairie houses," is created by the pinwheel-shaped design. Four long wings extend from a massive, three-story chimney, with five fireplaces on three floors, forming a brick core that rises 30 feet (9.1 meters) through three tiers of clerestory windows to a rooftop observatory. Surrounding this chimney is a large, octagonal space, the base of the "wigwam," as Wright nicknamed Wingspread's central living space. This 40- by 60-foot (12.2- by 18.3-meter) area contains four distinct zones on two levels, defined by shallow steps and ceiling height rather than by walls, and divided by the great chimney stack, the "sacred hearth," into separate spaces for the various domestic functions, reception area, family living, library, and dining room. This central space is one of Wright's finest interiors, finished in warm brick and oak rather than the darker American walnut used in the S.C. Johnson & Son Co. Administration Building, and bathed in light from the three bands of clerestory windows. Swirling out at different levels from this lofty central wigwam are the four wings, now converted into seminar rooms for the use of the current occupants, the Johnson Foundation, but which in Wright's original vision were zoned by function, like the central space. The south wing, or "zone," housed the kitchen, while the master-bedroom (north) wing extended over the eastern side of the living room to form a mezzanine, from which a spiral staircase ascended to the glazed observation tower on the roof. The west wing was assigned to guests and automobiles, while the east wing was the children's domain. The outer walls comprised tall, brick piers, separated by 15-foot-high (4.6-meter-high) windows that lent an air of transparency to the building. As Wright explained, "The building is orientated so that sunlight falls in all rooms and the ground plan shows a completely logical expression of the Zoned House …"

Wright felt that his pinwheel design was an ideal solution to the problems posed by a relatively featureless position: "This extended zoned-wing-plan lies, very much at home, quiet and integral with the prairie landscape which is, through it, made more significant and beautiful." Indeed, particularly tellingly, in view of his desire to harmonize "Mother Art" and Mother Nature, he spoke of the

Wingspread (above and left) was considered by the architect himself to be his best—and most expensive—house to date, and he described in *An Autobiography* how he "laid the house out on a scale befitting a young industrial prince of the Johnson line who lifelong had had just about everything he wanted."

Each of the four wings of the house creates an external space in the angle where it joins the central space, each one used for a different purpose: circular entrance driveway, terrace, formal garden, and pool (as seen in the view at left). The glass observatory that Wright added above the central fulcrum of the building can also be seen in the photograph at left.

The photograph above shows the cantilevered room that projects boldly from the end of the children's bedroom wing; inside, this light-filled space commands views over the grounds from its triple-aspect windows. The driveway is to the right in this view.

Tragically, the young second wife for whom Herbert F. Johnson had commissioned the house died before it was completed, and Wright had to guide the bereaved husband gently through the completion of the project for his young family. After serving for twenty years as a family home, the house was donated to the Johnson Foundation in 1959 for use as an educational and conference facility.

magical, transformational effect that the house exerted on its surroundings at Wind Point, a peninsula that juts into Lake Michigan: "The house did something remarkable to that site. The site was not stimulating before the house went up—but like developer poured over a negative, when you view the environment framed by the Architecture of the house from within, somehow, like magic—charm appears in the landscape and will be there wherever you looked. The site seems to come alive."

The interior fittings for Wingspread were as lavish as the plan. The central space acts as a focus for the four wings that seem to swing out from it. Three bands of clerestory windows circle the central roof and bathe the brick and oak tones of the living space in a rich light (above and opposite), and the enormous chimney soars up through the heart of the house. Wright placed trellises over the living-room windows, up which were trained grapevines, writing in *An Autobiography*: "In this case, especially, green growth will eventually claim its own."

# PURE GEOMETRY

The World War II era saw Wright spreading his own wings farther, venturing, for example, into South Carolina, where, in 1938, he designed Auldbrass House and Plantation buildings for Leigh Stevens on the banks of the Combahee River at Yemassee. Although this combination of a country retreat and gentleman's farm was not completed during either Wright's or Stevens's lifetime, it features a characteristic use of local material in the naturally finished cypress of the slanting exterior walls, combined with extensive use of glass. The main residence is planned on a six-sided module, and was intended to be connected to the other structures, including guest house, manager's quarters, and cottages, by a series of covered walkways, to form a working plantation. With their slanting uprights imitating the live oak on the property, and their natural finish, the various horizontal, one-story structures blend beautifully with their surroundings.

With the second house that Wright designed for Herbert Jacobs, in Middleton, Wisconsin, in 1943 (the first was a Usonian house, see page 79)—the first of the so-called "Solar Hemicycle" houses—the by now seventy-six-year-old architect moved into ever more innovative territory. For this commission, Wright had been asked to incorporate some means of making use of the thermal energy generated by the sun, and in responding to this request, he literally invited the power of nature into the home. In the case of the Jacobs's Solar Hemicycle house, Wright achieved this by incorporating the lower section of the rear of the house into the earth as a heat-conservation measure; at the front, the south-facing, two-story living space acts as a window-lined suntrap in winter (an overhanging roof ensures shade in summer) that curves around a circular, sunken, garden area; the bedrooms lie behind a balcony above.

Wright designed another house of this type in 1948 for Curtis Meyer. Situated in Galesburg, Michigan, it, too, is partly dug into a hillside and has a curved, inward-facing, window-rich living area, with the bedrooms being located on the floor above. This increased concern with circular shapes, seen in the design for the Solomon R. Guggenheim Museum, on which Wright was working throughout this period, as well as in his domestic architecture, has echoes in his earlier work, but also marks a new stage in Wright's continuing exploration of the ideas of plasticity and continuity of space and structure. And in the practical solutions that he developed to utilize thermal energy and conserve heat by natural means, he now seems some fifty years ahead of his time, speaking directly to the ecological conservation priorities of our own day.

The second house created for Herbert Jacobs (above) was Wright's first experiment with a "solar hemicycle." Set on an exposed hilltop site in Wisconsin, it consists of two-story circular segments, which, at the rear, are set into the hillside, protecting the building from the worst of the winter weather, while on the other side it opens to a beautiful view. Here a glassed façade gives on to a terrace, which is sunk 4 feet (1.3 meters) below the floor level, so as to give a sheltered space immediately outside.

In the living room at Auldbrass House and Plantation (opposite), the hexagonal module that forms the basis of the design is echoed in the furniture design; light filters in through a clerestory with carved, glazed openings.

The Kenneth Laurent House (opposite and above) was designed in interlocking circular segments as a single-story variant of the solar hemicycle, with the brief that it must be as accessible as possible for a wheelchair user. The curving garden room shown here gives easy access along its rear wall to the bedrooms, kitchen, entrance vestibule, and carport, while on the garden side it opens on to a terrace that curves the other way, creating the football shape of the design. The materials are common brick and cypress. Its simplicity of form, open, uncluttered design, and beautiful setting make this a tranquil space. At Wright's urging, the Laurents chose this site over the city lot that they originally had in mind.

Wright's experiments with geometric shapes in his pursuit of organic architecture took many forms. Homes predicated on diamond shapes feature in his work of the immediate postwar period, such as the houses that he designed, both in 1949 in Michigan, for Howard Anthony, at Benton Harbor, and Ward McCartney, in Kalamazoo. The home that he designed for Kenneth Laurent, in Rockford, Illinois, in 1949, however, reverts to the hemicycle principle. Laurent had approached Wright because, as he outlined in a letter to the architect on August 23, 1948, "… I am paralyzed from the waist down and by virtue of my condition I am confined to a wheelchair. This explains my need for a home as practical and sensible as your style of architecture denotes." Wright's solution was based on a "football-shaped" design, that is, two long arcs that meet at each end, one of which forms an outdoor terrace opening on to a slope leading down to Spring Creek, and the other, a loggia, with a bedroom being located at one end, a living room at the other, and a garden and pool in the space in the middle, all easily accessed by a wheelchair user.

A series of slender inverted pyramids contains the structural supports of this wing of the winter home (below) that Wright designed in 1954 in Paradise Valley, Arizona, for Harold Price, Sr., his client for the Price Tower. Its shade-providing roof appears to float, while the walls blend into the setting. The Ward McCartney House (1949, bottom) in Kalamazoo is based on a diamond-shaped grid.

The Norman Lykes House (opposite), on the edge of the Arizona desert on a steep slope overlooking Phoenix, is the last of Wright's domestic works. Its harmoniously curving shapes seem to curl themselves down into the surrounding landscape. The circular living and dining space is shaded by the generous roof, yet commands panoramic views over the city below.

And it was the circle that inspired Wright's last residential commission, the house that he designed for Norman Lykes, in Phoenix, Arizona, in 1959, and which he did not live to see completed. The ground plan comprises a series of circles or segments of circles, with five main radius centers. Set like a citadel on the edge of a canyon, the house's curving, concrete exterior, tinted desert pink, harmonizes so perfectly with the surrounding, harshly beautiful, desert landscape that it is as though it has grown organically from the earth. It illustrates that, at the end of his life, Frank Lloyd Wright was truly a master of melding "Mother Art" and Mother Nature.

# "THE UNITY OF ALL THINGS"

▣ ▣ ▣

## Sacred Spaces

▣ ▣ ▣

"A love of the beautiful is the divine spark in the soul of man never to be extinguished. ... This little meeting house ... is significant of the faith it represents. ... [It is] a tangible expression of what the Unitarian faith meant to me as a boy ... And that is the unity of all things. In the unity of all things comes the inspiration for the thing we call the Declaration of Independence, our faith—it is the very soul of a democracy and it is the centerline of everything we have. Here the feeling for reverence is something elemental to beauty and to religion, to the feeling of the human mind as it grows here on the earth."

—*An Autobiography*

*The Greek cross inscribed within a circle forms the motif that recurs throughout the design of the Annunciation Greek Orthodox Church (left), the last of Wright's sacred spaces to be built.*

# A NOBLE ROOM

In 1905 Frank Lloyd Wright was commissioned to design and build a new house of worship for his own Unitarian congregation in Oak Park, Illinois. On the subject of this, the Unity Temple, he later commented, "That was my first expression of this eternal idea which is at the center and core of all true modern architecture: … a new sense of space." Unity Temple set the pattern for the subsequent places of worship that Wright designed for American congregations of various faiths over the course of the following fifty years, combining as it did ancient concepts and symbols with modern materials to create, through the catalyst of Wright's unique vision and ingenious solutions, extraordinary buildings that made the spirit soar.

Many of Wright's sacred buildings were based on a dominant or recurrent shape or symbol, and in the case of Unity Temple, this was a cube. In *An Autobiography* Wright explained the evolution of his vision from its genesis: "The first idea was to keep a noble room for worship in mind, and let that sense of the great room shape the whole edifice. Let the room inside be the architecture outside." A "noble room" large enough to accommodate 400 worshippers was required, and yet funds were limited, which is why durable, versatile, and inexpensive concrete presented itself as the most appropriate construction material.

Wright's watercolor perspective (above) shows the temple at left and the social hall at right, connected by the entrance loggia, along the upper part of which is inscribed "For the worship of God and the service of man." The plain exterior, ornamented minimally in concrete, gives little clue of what may be found inside, beyond the "noble" form itself (opposite and top). A grid of roof beams inset with amber-colored skylights enables the walls to remain virtually windowless, for seclusion.

Next, Wright mused: "Why not make the wooden boxes or forms so the concrete could be cast in them as separate blocks and masses, these grouped about an interior space in some such way as to preserve this sense of the interior space, the great room, in the appearance of the whole building? And the block-masses might be left as themselves with no facing at all?" The roof, too, would be a slab of concrete, so that "This, reduced to simplest terms meant a building square in plan. That would make their temple a cube—a noble form in masonry."

And so the Unity Temple was constructed from liquid concrete poured into wooden forms. The edifice rose from a low, projecting base to a slab roof that jutted out over the rectangular masses and decorative columns of the façade. Once the concrete had set, the exterior surfaces, including the columns and other decorative elements, were washed clean to expose the small gravel aggregate, the finished result rather resembling coarse granite. The site adjoined streetcar tracks, making it noisy, but the thickness of the concrete walls muffled intrusive sounds.

In another dramatic contrast to the Gothic Revival church that had preceded it, the multilevel interior represented an entirely new kind of space for communal use, with its weight-bearing volumes being cleanly defined by slender, wooden uprights. The congregation's attention was directed by horizontal and vertical banding toward the pulpit—a projecting podium that gave the impression of uniting speaker and audience—and the abstract, vertical-lined

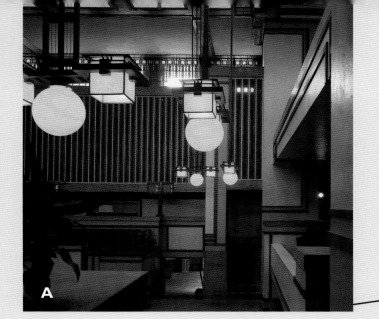

A

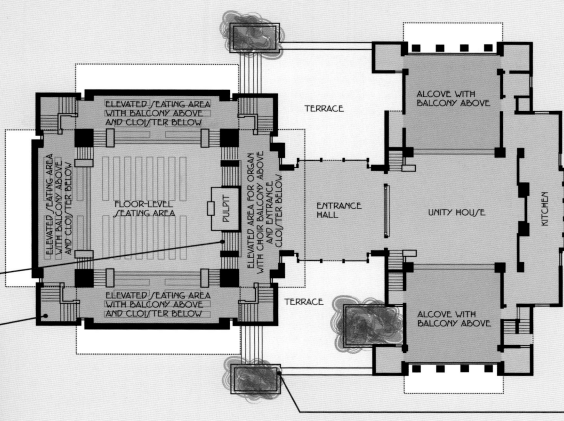

ELEVATED SEATING AREA
WITH BALCONY ABOVE
AND CLOISTER BELOW

TERRACE

ALCOVE WITH
BALCONY ABOVE

ELEVATED SEATING AREA
WITH BALCONY ABOVE
AND CLOISTER BELOW

FLOOR-LEVEL
SEATING AREA

PULPIT

ELEVATED AREA FOR ORGAN
WITH CHOIR BALCONY ABOVE
AND ENTRANCE
CLOISTER BELOW

ENTRANCE
HALL

UNITY HOUSE

KITCHEN

ELEVATED SEATING AREA
WITH BALCONY ABOVE
AND CLOISTER BELOW

TERRACE

ALCOVE WITH
BALCONY ABOVE

B

C

In America's first reinforced cast-concrete building, Wright "achieved a complete integration of material and space, a unity of place and experience," according to Robert McCarter. Yet its modern appearance belies the fact that Wright's design was inspired by ancient temple-building tradition. The plan reveals how he incorporated a Greek cross, defined by the temple's inset corner piers and projecting rooflines.

**A:** Entrances to the "noble room" are on either side of the pulpit; the geometric light fixtures, art-glass clerestory, and skylights (see B) illuminate the temple.
**B:** A grid of coffered, amber-colored skylights is built in above the worship space.
**C:** Unbroken walls below the clerestory provide privacy and quiet for the temple space. The hollow corner piers carry heating and ventilation ducts.
**D:** Concrete surfaces and pier-ornament detail, as seen from the entrance.

Wright explained in *An Autobiography* that he wanted the worship space (opposite) to be illuminated through the colored skylights with "the warmth of sunlight," creating "a sense of a happy cloudless day."

D

organ screen. Typical Wrightian touches included geometric hanging lamps that incorporated spheres and cubes and the art-glass clerestory, with natural lighting being filtered inside through the ribbons of windows and coffered, amber-colored skylights.

Loath, as Wright put it in his autobiography, to "spoil the simplicity of the room—the noble Room in the service of man for the worship of God" by incorporating space to accommodate secular activities, he constructed another room—Unity House—to the rear: "a separate building but harmonious with the Temple—the entrance to both to be the connecting link between them."

The Anne Pfeiffer Chapel (these pages) was the first building of the Florida Southern College campus, for which Wright designed the plan for a series of concrete structures that are stuccoed and painted brilliant white above first-story level, with bands of patterned blocks, inset with small blocks of colored glazing, below. The buildings are connected by low, shaded arcades that unify the design. Despite the chapel's apparently windowless appearance, congregants worship in a brightly lit space, with a vertical emphasis provided by the bell tower and its skylights, drawing the eye upward.

# A CHAPEL FOR TOMORROW

Wright turned again to concrete—specifically, reinforced cast concrete and sand-cast concrete blocks containing local limestone formed of indigenous shells and corals—for the Anne Pfeiffer Chapel that he designed for the Florida Southern College, in Lakeland, Florida, in 1938. This construction material matched that used for the buildings that, according to Wright's master plan, would surround the chapel, Dr. Ludd M. Spivey, the president of the college, having challenged Wright to design a "college of tomorrow" on a lake amid citrus groves.

Constructed on a hexagonal ground plan, the chapel's minimal ornamentation conveyed a powerful sense of unity, simplicity, and spiritual repose. Multilevel ceiling heights helped to define the angular form of the structure, in which the pulpit projected from a triangular stage toward the seating area. The bell tower soared beyond the choir loft's pierced-concrete screen, the skylight at its apex flooding the worship space below with light. And when viewed from afar, the bell tower's soaring verticality was a striking feature of a campus that was otherwise composed of low, horizontal buildings.

Robert McCarter commented in *Frank Lloyd Wright* that, for Wright, "light and a prismatic and geometric type of space were the architectural characteristics that allowed a place to achieve the sacred quality particular to worship." These interior perspectives of the Anne Pfeiffer Chapel manifest this idea, from the geometry of the main interior volume and ceilings to the patterns of light on and through its surfaces.

# A MODERN MEETING HOUSE

Wright was seventy-nine when, in 1946, he designed a meeting house for the First Unitarian Society of Madison—of which he was himself a member—in Shorewood Hills, Wisconsin. Here, the motif on which Wright based many of the building's symbolic and structural elements was an equilateral triangle, although the most eye-catching feature of the limestone-and-oak Unitarian Meeting House was the steeply angled, prow-shaped, copper-clad roof of the auditorium, which jutted boldly from a grassy slope, suggesting Noah's ark of salvation. The horizontally banded glass wall beneath its overhanging eave allowed natural light to illuminate the triangular auditorium that abutted a triangular hearth room at the rear for social gatherings, the two spaces thus forming a diamond shape. The warmth generated by the hearth was supplemented by heating pipes embedded in the red concrete floor.

A long, low wing, or loggia, extended from this, the heart of the meeting house, to the west, flanked by classrooms and leading to the living room. In his Unitarian Meeting House, Wright had created a light, warm, and welcoming, multipurpose space in which members could congregate, communicate, learn, and feel part of an inclusive community—the building and its community together becoming an embodiment of the "unity of all things."

Wright wanted a naturally beautiful and peaceful site for the Unitarian Meeting House, which looks out over fields toward a lake. He created a simple, light-filled sanctuary, in which the building's form is itself an expression of reverence, with its heavenward-pointing prow (shown above) taking the place of the symbolic steeple of traditional churches. Olgivanna, Wright's wife, said that its shape suggested hands held together in prayer. The interior view (opposite) shows how the seated congregants look toward the dazzling prow, with its central pulpit and a choir balcony above. By day the space is illuminated through the expanse of glass (right), and, by night, by the starlike, recessed ceiling lights.

# "A MOUNTAIN OF LIGHT"

Wright worked closely, and with respect, with the spiritual leaders and congregations for whom he undertook commissions for sacred spaces, studying the history, tenets, and iconography of their respective faiths to ensure that the buildings that he designed had spiritual significance and depth. For the Beth Sholom Synagogue (1953–59), in Elkins Park, a suburb of Philadelphia, Pennsylvania, Wright collaborated with Rabbi Mortimer J. Cohen, who envisioned the synagogue as resembling "a mountain of light," this "mountain" in turn symbolizing Mount Sinai, where the Ten Commandments were revealed to Moses. That is why this sacred structure is pyramidal in form.

Glowing like a beacon at night (above) and resembling a solid peak by day (opposite), the "mountain of light" is also a masterpiece of geometry and engineering. The translucent surfaces—neither quite walls nor windows—are layered, not only contributing insulation, but filtering light so that the interior (previous pages) has an otherworldly quality, simultaneously enclosed and open. The pyramid of structural members obviates the need for internal supports, freeing the worship space and giving emphasis to the striking, hovering chandelier. Outside, seven menorah details adorn each of the main beams, as seen in profile on both the day and night views on these pages.

Constructed on a hexagonal base, the elevation forms a massive, tentlike structure suspended from a 160-ton (145,150-kilogram) tripod of steel and concrete. This resemblance to a tent is significant, too, for it evokes the tents and tabernacles that were used by the nomadic Jews of the Old Testament period. The menorah motif on the steel tripod that ascends to the roofline recurs throughout the exterior and interior of the temple. The huge, triangular canopy that projects over the main entrance represents hands joined in blessing, protecting the congregation.

Within, above the entrance level (which housed meeting rooms, bridal suites, and other rooms dedicated to the synagogue's communal functions), the interior sloped gently toward its focal point—an unobstructed sanctuary, at the center of which was the sacred ark that contained the Torah. More than one thousand worshippers could be accommodated in the prayer hall that surrounded the sanctuary, seated beneath a colored-glass, winged-triangle chandelier that represented inexpressible attributes of the Divine. Walls of aluminum, glass, and fiberglass filtered natural light into the sanctuary during daylight hours, and when viewed from outside by night, the interior lighting caused the whole structure to glow. "Here you have a coherent statement of worship," wrote Wright, in a letter to Rabbi Cohen that accompanied the initial plans for the synagogue.

# WRIGHT'/ "LITTLE /OFIA"

The Annunciation Greek Orthodox Church (1955–61), at Wauwatosa, Wisconsin, was the last sacred space that Wright designed. When planning it, the by now eighty-eight-year-old architect was advised by his third wife, Olgivanna Lazovich, a native of the Balkan country of Montenegro who had been raised in the Greek Orthodox faith. Wright was also inspired by his own knowledge of Byzantine architecture, which he admired deeply, and, indeed, he nicknamed the Greek Orthodox church that he was designing his "little Sofia," in reference to the monumental Hagia Sofia in Constantinople (now Istanbul, Turkey).

As in his previous commissions for places of worship, Wright used faith-appropriate, recurring motifs for the Annunciation Greek Orthodox Church, in this case, the Greek cross (whose four arms are of equal lengths) and the dome. The ground plan of this concrete building was consequently based on a Greek cross within a circle, a symbol that could be seen elsewhere in the building, such as in the anodized-aluminum iconostasis, or icon screen, in front of the altar, whose gold accents evoked a traditional feature of Greek Orthodox iconography. The precast-, perforated-concrete sunscreen that encircled the roofline like a crown when viewed from the outside was sharply pointed, recalling the paramount Byzantine theme of Christ Triumphant, as seen in icons and mosaics at, for instance, the Hagia Sofia. Four cast-concrete piers supported the bowl-shaped balcony, which provided seating and was ringed by glazed, bow-shaped arches that let in natural light, the shape of these windows being echoed by that of the portal at the top of the steps that worshippers ascended before entering the church. And surmounting the balcony was the shallow dome of the roof, which measured 106 feet (32 meters) in diameter. The whole is a place of worship that appears to belong to the space age in its streamlined form, yet embodies in its very geometry the ancient traditions and tenets of the faith that inspired it.

The reflections (opposite) emphasize how the variously sized arcs of the dome, the bowl-shaped lower part of the structure, the balcony-level windows, and the trim above (top right) both interact and unify all the elements into a simple, integrated whole. The statuesque circle enclosing the Greek cross (right) is a planar version of the church's form in three dimensions: the four corner piers of the building are the arms that hold up the disk-shaped body. The circle is repeated inside in the shape of the balcony, as well as in ornamentation (opposite, top). Wright's creation, marrying ancient and modern, is pure and timeless.

# "STYLE ITSELF"

□ □ □

# Late Masterpieces

□ □ □

"Organic architecture *is a new idea of what constitutes a building.* It introduces wholly new values into building. An entirely new ethic—and esthetic—comes to life when the building is so conceived as intrinsic, as the result of the nature of materials, tools, situations, and the human beings it shelters. Wherever it is honestly built, you may see a new countenance, the countenance of truth emerging.

"Architecture is primarily interior; *of* the thing, not *on* it. It is not a dead aspect of style but *style* itself, bearing ever fresh form, like all living things in nature."

—Article in *House Beautiful*, July 1953
(Reprinted in *Collected Writings*, Vol. 5)

*Wright began work on his design for the Solomon R. Guggenheim Museum (left), New York, New York, in 1943, but continued to develop it over the next sixteen years. Now his best-known structure, the museum was only completed after his death. In* Frank Lloyd Wright: The Masterworks, *Bruce Brooks Pfeiffer called it "in many ways … the apotheosis of Wright's concepts of organic architecture."*

Wright's designs of the 1930s, including Fallingwater of 1935–37, the S.C. Johnson & Son Co. Administration Building (Johnson Wax) of 1936, and Taliesin West (from 1937), are now rightly recognized as major achievements and hugely influential in the history of U.S. architecture, but at the time the architect's career was by no means flourishing. He was not involved in the three major building projects of the decade—the Rockefeller Center in New York City, New York (1929–34), the Chicago Fair of 1933, and the New York World's Fair of 1939—and, already well into his sixties, might have been assumed to have been fading into retirement. It was the commission for the Solomon R. Guggenheim Museum in New York City in 1943 that not only offered him the opportunity to make the ultimate statement of his theory of organic architecture, but also opened the door to a much wider range of projects and commissions for his practice during the postwar period.

# A TEMPLE OF SPIRIT

Arguably Wright's most famous and iconic building, the Guggenheim, with its characteristic spiraling ramp and swelling profile, marks the culmination of his later work, combining the structural plasticity and spatial continuity of Fallingwater with the top-lit definition of the S.C. Johnson & Son Co. Administration Building. His long-held principle of natural growth "from within upwards" is reflected in the Guggenheim's treelike columns and curved elements. Its circular form, "the spiral, organic process," had first appeared in the visionary project for an "automobile objective and planetarium" sketched for Chicago entrepreneur Gordon Strong as early as 1924–25, a circular, mountaintop construction with a double spiral of external ramps for the newly fashionable automobile. But at the same time, Wright's final design for the Guggenheim uses steel-reinforced concrete to give the exterior a streamlined, purely sculptural form, devoid of surface decoration and representing a welding of architecture and engineering into a new form of organic whole.

In an article of June 1958 about the Solomon R. Guggenheim Museum (right), Wright wrote that its "walls and spaces, inside and outside, are one in substance and effect." He described how the surfaces form a "giant spiral for a well-defined purpose: a new unity between beholder, painting and architecture." This integration of art, setting, and person is fleshed out in his interior perspective (page 158), which shows how a painting would be "free to become itself; to be master of its own allotted space."

THE MASTERPIECE

The commission came about relatively fortuitously. Solomon Guggenheim (1861–1949), the hugely wealthy fourth son of the industrialist Meyer Guggenheim, had long been a collector of traditional Old Masters, but from the mid-1920s, turned his attention to twentieth-century European abstract art, being then under the influence of the German-born artist Baroness Hilla Rebay von Ehrenweisen, who had exhibited as a member of the avant-garde *Der Sturm* (German for "The Storm") group alongside Paul Klee, Wassily Kandinsky, Franz Marc, Max Ernst, and others. In 1937 the Solomon R. Guggenheim Foundation was established in order to make the collection available to the public, and by 1939 more than 700 paintings were on display in a remodeled townhouse. Rebay was the curator of this temporary Museum of Non-Objective Painting.

Guggenheim and Rebay had already decided that a permanent museum was needed, and it was Rebay who first approached Wright by letter in June 1943. Her account of the project might have been assumed to have appealed to Wright: "functionalism does not agree with non-objectivity … I want a temple of spirit, a monument! And your help to make it possible." But the architect's response was initially offhand: he was reluctant to go to New York and, assuming that Rebay was a man, suggested that "he and his wife" might "run down" to Taliesin for a weekend. Rebay, however, responded firmly that "Mr. Guggenheim is 82 years old and we have no time to lose … Please come to New York." By mid-June Wright was indeed in New York to meet both Rebay and Guggenheim himself, and by June 29 a contract had been drawn up, covering both site and building at a cost of no more than $1 million.

Wright initially favored a hilltop site outside the city for the museum, overlooking the Hudson River, so that the museum could be "a new type of Treasury for works of art, one that would be a haven of refuge for city dwellers." Rebay and Guggenheim, however, both wanted an accessible, high-profile, city-center location, and by mid-March 1944, they had decided on a lot on the corner of Fifth Avenue at 89th Street. This was planned from the outset to include an auditorium, offices, classrooms, and studios for guest artists, in addition to the exhibition gallery. It seems that the collection was intended to be regarded as more or less complete when Guggenheim died (and, indeed, an adjunct to his will specified that the foundation was to make no additions to the collection without Rebay's specific approval).

Wright's brief was to create a space that both actively reflected the revolutionary nature of Guggenheim's collection as a whole and also permitted the viewer to follow the development of a painter or a movement over time: a space that expressed both totality and change. The standard rectilinear museum plan of strings of rooms and corridors was inimical to such a purpose, and Wright rose superbly to the challenge. He outlined his new scheme to Rebay and Guggenheim as "one extended expansive well proportioned floor space from bottom to top …" with "no stops anywhere," stressing that the design would make paintings and architecture work together to form a unified environment. He described it in a letter to Rebay as a "modern version of the ziggurat," musing, "we can use it either top side down or down side top."

Wright remarked, in his 1958 essay on the museum, that "Here for the first time architecture appears plastic, one floor flowing into another (more like sculpture) instead of the more usual superimposition of stratified layers."

His comment illustrates how his vision of imaginative and fresh, organic design led him to ever greater creativity in engineering, too. The museum's sculptural interior (page 159) and the art within were intended to synthesize like "an uninterrupted, beautiful symphony."

The revised plans and model were completed during the summer of 1945, and in the event, the version that Wright actually showed was "down side top," an inverted ziggurat top-lit by a shallow glass dome, with the main gallery formed of a 1320-foot-long (402-meter-long) cantilevered ramp that descended in a continuous, spiraling curve from the roof. The huge skylight would provide an unusually generous abundance of natural light, while the outward-sloping walls approximated, so Wright said, the angle at which a canvas slopes when standing on an easel to be painted.

This basic concept remained unchanged throughout a painfully long-drawn-out period of revisions and negotiations, necessitated partly by soaring cost estimates and partly by the requirements of the New York Building Commission, which registered thirty-two building-code violations in the initial plans. The building permit was finally issued in March 1956, but in the meantime, complications had arisen due to Guggenheim's death in 1949 and Rebay's gradual withdrawal and final resignation from the museum in 1952. The museum's new director, James Johnson Sweeney, significantly changed the terms of the commission, in accordance with his vision of an expanding collection and a schedule of temporary exhibitions across the whole range of modern art, with the associated administrative and curatorial space that this necessitated.

The version finally built reflects a certain amount of inevitable compromise in order to achieve this revised brief, yet Wright's basic vision holds true. The spiraling form of the exterior is a direct expression of the internal space; the inverted-cone shape, with the larger spirals at the top, leaves ground space for an airy entryway, parking, and sculpture gardens. At the southern end of the site, the second level spreads out and flows across the frontage, creating a fixed space for the Guggenheim's permanent holdings, while at the northern end, a subsidiary unit nestles against the cone and houses staff offices.

Sweeney had a particular problem with the sloping angle at which Wright intended the pictures be seen, a criticism also voiced by some leading artists, including Willem de Kooning and Robert Motherwell, who wrote to the board of trustees in 1956 condemning the building's "callous disregard for the fundamental rectilinear frame of reference necessary for the adequate visual contemplation of works of art." Wright argued that, on the contrary, paintings placed against a tilted, outward-curving wall would be liberated from their background and would be seen as objects in their own right. However, he agreed to lop 30 inches (76 centimeters) off the overhang before construction finally began later in 1956. Sweeney, for his part, continued to maintain that the paintings should be mounted on tripods and suspended in space to compensate for the angle of the wall. This would have the effect of detaching the paintings from the architectural frame that Wright had conceived for them, provoking the architect's fierce resistance to the idea. Wright died in April 1959, however, after which Sweeney's proposal carried the day.

When the building opened in October 1959, just six months after Wright's death, the public reaction was immediate and positive, with nearly 3000 people waiting in line to view it on the first day, and another 10,000 the following Sunday. Yet critics and professionals were less than unanimous in their approval, with some hailing its daring spatial and sculptural form, but others regarding it as an attack on the arts, "an architecture totally irrelevant to its purpose." The editor of *Art News* was more even-handed: "It takes Wright's kind of egomania to smash the pattern … perhaps the idea of a museum will now be thought about again, and as a new concept."

It is ironic, then, that in many ways, the Guggenheim anticipated developments in painting and sculpture during the decade following its opening, and, indeed, stimulated some artists to create radical new work specifically for its challenging space. It has become the showcase for artworks that break the mold in which they were formed as surely as Wright's design broke the architectural mold in which it was conceived.

That Wright's "temple of spirit" is as much a work of art as any piece displayed within it is evident in this view of the rotunda, crowned by its elegant skylight (opposite). In this photograph, the spiraling ramp wall is clad with brilliantly reflective stainless steel that warps the light playfully, seeming to liquefy the entire structure. Only in the negative space is the appearance of a smooth surface preserved. The installation by leading architect Frank O. Gehry (who designed the Guggenheim Museum Bilbao, in Spain) "both transforms and emphasizes the essence of Wright's structure," noted curator Thomas Krens in the catalog for "The Art of the Motorcycle" exhibition for which it was created in 1998.

# THE TREE TOWER

The 1950s brought a series of public commissions for Wright that offered a range of new opportunities for him to give expression to ideas that he had long been harboring and developing. He was convinced that the egalitarian culture that he termed "Usonian" would spontaneously emerge in the United States from the upheavals of raw capitalism. This belief found expression not only in domestic architecture, but also in the unrealized Broadacre City project, a visionary and agrarian-based response to Le Corbusier's revolutionary proposal for a contemporary city planned around the imagery of modern technology that had had its genesis during the 1920s.

One of the first of these new commissions was the dual-function tower, combining both office and residential space, that Wright designed for the H.C. Price Company in 1952 as the corporate headquarters for the local oil-pipeline and chemical firm that Harold C. Price had founded in Bartlesville, Oklahoma. This nineteen-story tower is the only fully realized skyscraper design by Wright, and he described it as "the tree that escaped the crowded forest," in reference both to its location—on the open Oklahoma prairie—and to its construction. For a central core, like a trunk or taproot, holds four elevator shafts anchored—rooted—in a deep, central foundation, while the floors are cantilevered from the trunk in four quadrants, resembling branches.

The basic design idea for the tower was one that had developed and matured over time. Wright had worked on a similar project for a tower apartment block as part of his St. Mark's-in-the-Bouwerie scheme in New York City in 1929, an early expression of Usonian principles that had come to nothing following the onset of the Depression years. Wright considered the St. Mark's tower to be a new form of urban architecture and took the opportunity to attack the International Style as it developed in New York as "man-eating skyscrapers, all tall but seeking false monumental mass … this utter contradiction of structure and idea is what is most destructive everywhere in New York." By contrast he described his ideal tall building: "lightness, openness and tenuous strength combined should be its building characteristics … the whole so designed and the fabric so insulated as to emphasize the pattern of the structure itself and not belie the way it was actually built."

The Price Tower is unmistakably the offspring of these ideas, articulated in Wright's autobiography and made manifest at last in the Midwest during the 1950s. The building was planned on a module consisting of a 2½-foot (76-centimeter) equilateral parallelogram, creating a polygonal grid that is essentially diamond-shaped. This dictated the position of all exterior walls, interior partitions and doors, and even the built-in furniture. At each level the quadrant plan is divided into one duplex apartment and three office suites. The floor area increases substantially as the tower rises, again recalling the spreading canopy of a tree. Toward the top of the tower, on the sixteenth floor, the highest duplex apartment had a buffet and kitchen, as well as outside terraces with planting areas.

In the Price Tower (opposite), Wright realized a concept that had been in his mind for many years; the complex layout and external articulation of this skyscraper successfully transforms a multicellular building into an individual, organic whole. The reception floor of one of the apartments (left), showing the breakfast bar with a mezzanine floor above.

The central concrete spine that supports the building penetrates the façade, breaking it up into a rhythm of planes and angles (right), while bands of copper-clad windows (detail above) give the vertical tower a contrasting horizontal accent. Each floor holds three office suites (opposite) and one level of a duplex apartment. The bronze parallelogram on the office floor (opposite) bears the H.C. Price Company logo; the grid was based on this shape.

On the seventeenth floor is a small, central office space, with a mural signed by Wright, as well as a living room forming the upper floor of the duplex. Price's own office was on the nineteenth floor.

Despite its urban location and function, this is quintessentially organic architecture. The effect of the sharply angled ground plan is to create a prismatic, faceted structure, a complete contrast to the steel-framed, curtain-walled, "man-eating" New York skyscrapers so roundly condemned by Wright. Reinforced concrete forms the central core of the Price Tower and emerges at the top and bottom of the design to assert its function, while the outer walls hang from the cantilevered floors and are clad in copper louvers, with copper-faced parapets and gold-tinted glass borne on an armature of floating planes forming a skin on the concrete core. The articulation of the façades alternates between a horizontal and a vertical emphasis, and no two are identical. Continuous, green-copper mullions, concrete bands, decorative panels, and projecting sunshades are arranged in a sequence of subtly varying combinations so that the tower presents a different appearance from every angle.

The exterior of the Kalita Humphreys Theater (opposite) is formed of a series of geometric shapes in poured concrete, with the great, circular stage drum rising dominantly above the flat, rectangular forms below. The entrance balustrade at the base of the design echoes the circular motif, and a heavy cantilevered slab shades the forecourt. A clerestory can be seen under the projecting eaves in the photograph opposite.

The internal design is equally innovative, with its cast-concrete walls, pigmented-concrete floors, aluminum-trimmed windows and doors, and patinated and distressed copper panels. The principal internal decorative motif is the equilateral triangle, pleasingly echoing the angular floor plan. The angled walls and built-in furniture are based on fractions or multiples of this triangular module, and all of the furniture was custom-designed, with Wright's usual painstaking eye for every detail apparent: even the lighting fixtures and ventilation grilles are based upon the triangular form.

In the Price Tower (below), Wright designed every detail of the furnishings, fittings, light fixtures, and ornamentation, inside and outside, to echo the geometry of the floor plan. In this view there are no right angles defining the boundaries of the space, but a series of acute and obtuse angles formed at the junctions of walls, balustrades, ceilings, and floor. These are the angles inherent in the parallelogram of the grid, and sections of this basic shape are expressed in the inset ceiling-light fixtures, as well as in the furnishings. The Price Tower was one of seventeen of Wright's designs to be chosen by the American Institute of Architects as exemplars of his contribution to American culture.

# PURE THEATER

Like the Price Tower, the Dallas Theater Center (1955), in Dallas, Texas, which is also known as the Kalita Humphreys Theater, is one of a kind, being the only commissioned theater completed from Wright's designs. It does, however, have clear links with earlier theater projects going back at least as far as Wright's "New Theater" proposal of 1932. In all of these, the main innovation was the handling of the proscenium and stage. While Wright was not the first to experiment with theater in the round, he brought his characteristic ingenuity to the challenge of deconstructing the traditional "picture frame," and the relation between the auditorium, stage, and backstage areas shows the same interpenetration of space at various levels that is a feature of so much of his architecture.

The other feature that these earlier designs share with the Dallas Theater Center is the omission of the usual fly tower. Instead Wright situated the usually overhead equipment underground, along with storage space, classrooms, and workshops. The sets rise to stage level on tracks ascending spiral ramps from a set-building workshop in the basement. Since there was no restriction on space in any of these projects (and the Dallas Theater Center was set into the hillside on a substantial site), it would appear that this innovation reflects the same fascination with curving ramps for their own sake that is evident in the S.C. Johnson & Son Co. Administration Building and the Solomon R. Guggenheim Museum.

When it opened in December 1959, the Dallas Theater Center was an imposing, six-sided, poured-concrete, cantilevered structure consisting of bold, interlinked, geometric forms, with a dramatic, multilevel roofline. The focus of the design, both inside and out, is the circular stage drum, which rises well above the rest of the concrete mass and contains the 40-foot-diameter (12-meter-diameter) circular stage, which in turn holds a 32-foot-diameter (10-meter-diameter) turntable. This turntable is divided into three sections so that while one set is on stage, one can be struck, and one is ready to be set up for the next scene, all at the same time. The stage is flanked by wide side stages and balconies, substantially extending the potential performing space. The seating, arranged in stepped rows, wraps around the central hemicycle in a 180-degree arc. The result was described by one drama critic as "one of Wright's happiest solutions to a practical problem." Performing and viewing spaces merge seamlessly into an uninterrupted whole, and actors and audience are united in a single, shared experience.

# A RING OF HILLS

The commission for the Marin County Civic Center and Post Office in May 1957, proposed for a site in San Rafael, California, provided Wright with a further opportunity to design a public building for the more democratic state of which he dreamed. Just across the Golden Gate Bridge from San Francisco, Marin County had shared in the area's postwar boom and population growth. By the 1950s the administrative needs of the area had outstripped the facilities available in San Rafael, and the decision was taken to group all of the county offices, library, law courts, and jail within a complex that would also hold an auditorium, recreational facilities, and county fairgrounds.

The location chosen was a large, flat, accessible area of former farmland ringed by softly rolling, golden hills, and Wright's response to the site was immediate. "The good building," he told the locals in a talk when he came to sign the contract, "is not one that hurts the landscape but is one that makes the landscape more beautiful than it was before that building was built. Now in Marin County you have one of the most beautiful landscapes I have seen … I am here to help make the buildings of this country characteristic of the beauty of the county."

Wright's plan for the Marin County site was a characteristic combination of twentieth-century technology and materials, closely integrated with the landscape, and equally characteristically intended to serve the people in the noblest way. The related images of bridge and water dominate the conception in an echo of the great Roman aqueducts that Wright had admired during his European travels. At its heart is the use that Wright made of the three low hills on the southern part of the site and his determination to "bridge these hills with graceful arches." The main, elongated, two-pronged civic center consists of the 560-foot-long (171-meter-long) administration building and the 850-foot-long (259-meter-long) hall of justice, which link and merge into two hills at their farther ends, and which meet at a 120-degree angle on a third hill.

This junction is the focal point and centerpiece of the whole site, and Wright marked it with a shallow-domed, circular library building crowning the hill. A hilltop garden serves as an outdoor terrace and forms a prow overlooking an artificial lake and the fairgrounds in the valley. The dome of the library is reflected in a circular fountain that flows into a curvilinear channel through the retaining wall of the prow to feed the lake below, forming a link between the civic center proper and the various facilities associated with the fairgrounds. Above the terrace soars a 172-foot-tall (52-meter-tall) pylon, which Wright intended to act as a transmitting tower, and which adds a dramatic exclamation point with its stepped, ziggurat-style, decorative bands.

Both wings are four stories high, but sited on different levels, so that the fourth floor of the hall of justice is level with the second floor of the administration building, giving a sense of rhythm and movement to the overall concept. The wings are simply constructed in steel-reinforced concrete, and the construction technique makes use of segmentation and expansion joints so that the center, which lies in the region of the San Andreas Fault, should be able to withstand a major seismic shock. Wide arches at the ground level support the two buildings as they span roadways and spring from hill to hill. At the second and third levels, the arches progressively narrow, and, despite their structural appearance, are, in fact, nonsupporting, instead being pendants, hanging from the slab edge to form a series of arcs that shade the balconies on to which the glass walls of the office floors open.

The successive series of arches stepping up the long façade of the Marin County Civic Center (above) give a swiftly flowing rhythm to the bold, flat structure, while the soft color of the concrete strikes a contrasting note to the blue vaults and dome of the roof. A golden spire breaks up the horizontal flow. The aluminum cornice decorating the roof's edge, with its curves and spheres, both shades the offices below and frames the rolling landscape that inspired the center's design (opposite, below); the arcs are picked up in the interior detailing (opposite, above). Water plays an essential role in the Marin design. This curving channel flowing down to the lake below appears to have been drawn out of the surrounding hills and enhances the building's link with its environment (right).

The fourth level is simply a series of oculi, tucked under the overhanging, vaulted roof, which in turn consists of a thin concrete shell sprayed with a blue plastic membrane. The fascia edge of the roof is decorated on both sides with a gold-coated aluminum cornice that features an extended pattern of spheres, resembling drops of water. This cornice acts as a sunshade for the windows that are set back behind and below, and also hides the inevitable variations in such a long roofline by breaking it up into a dynamic pattern through which the sun casts dramatically curving shadows.

Down the center of each wing runs a central atrium or mall, landscaped and planted at ground level. Every office in the complex opens either on to the garden mall or toward the lake and distant hills that lie beyond—a stirring affirmation of the complex's harmonious integration with its landscape setting. Wright had originally intended the atria to be open to the sky, but in a concession to the need for protection from the weather, later designed the gently domed glass roof that now curves over the calm and sheltered space below.

The soaring, triangular, golden spire that Wright designed to house a radio-transmitting antenna (above and opposite) strikes a bold, vertical note in the predominantly horizontal layout of the Marin County Civic Center. Rising skyward above the shallow-domed library building, it provides a stark contrast to the latter's low, curving profile. The counterpoint created by these two structures forms the primary focus of the complex as a whole, the central pivot on which the extended wings turn. Both also echo the theme, dear to Wright's heart, of public service: the library building offers information and learning through printed media, the tower, communication and learning through broadcast media. Wright held strong views about the value of democracy as the ideal form of government, local government included, calling it "the aristocracy of the man, the individual," who, through enlightened social and educational policies, is given the means and the opportunity to better himself through personal achievement.

# PERFORMANCE ART

The Grady Gammage Memorial Auditorium at Arizona State University, Tempe, Arizona, is Wright's final nonresidential design. It was planned as a center for performing arts just before the architect's death in 1959, and as a simplified version of the opera-house design that formed part of the major Baghdad project that had been commissioned by the Iraqi government, but was never realized. Completed from Wright's unfinished plans and built posthumously between 1962 and 1964, it is unmistakably from the master's hand, the design being dominated, both internally and externally, by a flowing rhythm of circles and arches, with the sandy-rose coloring of the building materials subtly echoing the appearance of the surrounding desert landscape.

The Grady Gammage Memorial Auditorium was conceived as two intersecting, circular units, the larger one holding the auditorium, lobbies, and ramps, the smaller one housing the stage, dressing rooms, workshops, teaching areas, and offices. The auditorium is on three levels, with the middle one, the grand tier, being suspended in front of the rear wall on a 145-foot-long (44-meter-long) steel beam, which gives the area below the acoustic quality of an open space. The wide stage has a steel acoustic shell that can either be adjusted for a full orchestra and choir or be collapsed and stored during theatrical performances.

The exterior wall of the auditorium is composed of an arcade of fifty slim, concrete columns rising to support the outer roof, each arch embellished with curving elements that resemble the drawn curtains of a traditional, proscenium-arched stage. The external walls are made of brick and Marblecrete, a composition material resembling marble, and were given a glowing, desert-sand finish; a similar color scheme dominates the brick-and-plaster interior. The complex is reached by means of 200-foot-long (61-meter-long) ramped, pedestrian walkways that lead the audience from the sunken gardens and parking lot and that are lit by globe-shaped lanterns suspended in a series of copper-colored arches.

In the Grady Gammage Memorial Auditorium (these pages), Wright played yet another creative variation on two of the predominant themes in his work: his fascination with geometric forms—in this case, curves and spheres—and his overriding concern to integrate his architecture with its environment. Beauty, Wright mused in his last written words, is vital to us, and creative architecture, "the greatest proof of [the] immortal soul." Believing the spiritual and artistic to be essential elements of the human experience, he declared that "Architecture lies deep as the basic culture of all civilizations, serving and served by the arts of sculpture, painting and music."

THE WRIGHT EXPERIENCE
172

# INDEX

Page numbers in *italics* refer to illustrations and captions.

# BIBLIOGRAPHY

⊡ ⊡ ⊡ ⊡ ⊡ ⊡ ⊡ ⊡ ⊡ ⊡ ⊡

Blake, Peter. *Frank Lloyd Wright.* Harmondsworth: Penguin Books Ltd, 1963.

Ehrlich, Doreen. *Frank Lloyd Wright Glass.* London: B.T. Batsford, 2001.

Hanks, David A. *The Decorative Designs of Frank Lloyd Wright.* New York: Dover Publications, 1999.

Hart, Spencer. *Wright Rooms.* New York: Chartwell, 1998.
___. *The Wright Space.* San Diego: Thunder Bay, 2000 (reissued: Barnes & Noble, 2005, 2007.)

Heinz, Thomas. *Frank Lloyd Wright Field Guide.* Evanston: Northwestern University Press, 2004.

Hitchcock, Henry-Russell. *In the Nature of Materials: The Buildings of Frank Lloyd Wright, 1887–1941.* New York: Da Capo Press, 1975 (first published by Duell, Sloan and Pearce, 1942).

Hoffmann, Donald. *Frank Lloyd Wright's Dana House.* New York: Dover Publications, 1996.
___. *Frank Lloyd Wright's Robie House.* New York: Dover Publications, 1985.
___. *Understanding Frank Lloyd Wright's Architecture.* New York: Dover Publications, 1995.

Huxtable, Ada Louise. *Frank Lloyd Wright* (Penguin Lives Series*).* New York: Viking, 2004.

Izzo, Alberto, and Gubitosi, Camillo. *Frank Lloyd Wright: Three Quarters of a Century of Drawings.* London: Academy Editions, 1976, reprinted 1981.

Kaufmann, Edgar, Jr. *Fallingwater: A Frank Lloyd Wright Country House.* New York: Abbeville Press, 1986.

Levine, Neil. *The Architecture of Frank Lloyd Wright.* Princeton: Princeton University Press, 1996.

Lind, Carla. *The Wright Style: The Interiors of Frank Lloyd Wright.* London: Thames & Hudson, 1992.

Lipman, Jonathan. *Frank Lloyd Wright and the Johnson Wax Buildings.* New York: Rizzoli, 1986.

McCarter, Robert. *Frank Lloyd Wright.* New York and London: Phaidon Press, 1997.
___. *Frank Lloyd Wright* (Critical Lives Series*).* London: Reaktion Books, 2006.

Pfeiffer, Bruce Brooks, *Frank Lloyd Wright.* Cologne: Taschen, 2002.
___. *Frank Lloyd Wright Drawings: Masterworks from the Frank Lloyd Wright Collection.* New York: Harry N. Abrams, 1996.
___. *Frank Lloyd Wright, Master Builder.* London: Thames & Hudson, 1997.
___. *Frank Lloyd Wright: The Masterworks.* New York: Rizzoli, 1993.

Reisley, Roland. *Usonia, New York: Building a Community with Frank Lloyd Wright.* New York: Princeton Architectural Press, 2001.

Secrest, Meryle. *Frank Lloyd Wright.* New York: Alfred A. Knopf, 1992.

Smith, Kathryn. *Frank Lloyd Wright: Hollyhock House and Olive Hill.* New York: Rizzoli, 1992.

Sommer, Robin Langley. *Frank Lloyd Wright: American Architect for the 20th Century.* New York: Smithmark, 1993
___. *Frank Lloyd Wright: A Gatefold Portfolio.* New York: Barnes & Noble, 1997.

Stipe, Margo. *Frank Lloyd Wright Interactive Portfolio.* Philadelphia: Running Press, 2004.

Storrer, William Allin. *The Architecture of Frank Lloyd Wright: A Complete Catalog.* Chicago: University of Chicago Press, 2002.
___. *The Frank Lloyd Wright Companion.* Chicago: University of Chicago Press, 1993.

Tafel, Edgar. *About Wright.* New York: Wiley, 1995.

Twombly, Robert C. *Frank Lloyd Wright: His Life and his Architecture.* New York: John Wiley, 1979.

Wright, Frank Lloyd. *Ausgeführte Bauten und Entwürfe von Frank Lloyd Wright.* Berlin: Ernst Wasmuth, 1910.
___. *An Autobiography.* Revised edition. Petaluma, California: Pomegranate Communications, Inc., 1943. In association with the Frank Lloyd Wright Foundation.
___. *Drawings and Plans of Frank Lloyd Wright: The Early Period (1893–1909).* New York: Dover Publications, 1985. (English edition of the Wasmuth drawings and introduction.)
___. *Frank Lloyd Wright Collected Writings.* Edited by Bruce Brooks Pfeiffer. Vol. 1 (1894–1930). New York: Rizzoli, 1992.
___. *Frank Lloyd Wright Collected Writings.* Edited by Bruce Brooks Pfeiffer. Vol. 3 (1931–39). New York: Rizzoli, 1993.
___. *Frank Lloyd Wright Collected Writings.* Edited by Bruce Brooks Pfeiffer. Vol. 5 (1951–59). New York: Rizzoli, 1995.
___. "The Art and Craft of the Machine." 1901. Reprinted in *Collected Writings*, Vol. 1.
___. "In the Cause of Architecture." 1927–28. Reprinted in *Collected Writings*, Vol. 1.
___. *The Disappearing City.* 1932. Reprinted in *Collected Writings*, Vol. 3.
___. *The Natural House.* New York: Horizon Press, 1954.
___. *A Testament.* New York: Bramhall House, 1957.

# ACKNOWLEDGMENTS

⊡ ⊡ ⊡ ⊡ ⊡ ⊡ ⊡ ⊡ ⊡ ⊡ ⊡ ⊡ ⊡

The publisher would like to thank the contributors, the photographers, and others who supplied images (see below), as well as the following individuals who have assisted in the preparation of this book: Kathryn Smith, for invaluable editorial input; Lynne Arany, who contributed to the timeline; Clare Haworth-Maden for editorial work and the index; Monica Korab, Elaine Rocheleau, Janet Hicks, Alessandra Pinzani, Ryan Jensen, and Kim Bush, for their help with photo selections and image administration; Roland Reisley, Bob Schweitzer, Peter Murray, Ron Scherubel, Milton Robinson, Rebecca Christina Lochhead, Peter Norton, and Cynthia Barrett for their time and assistance; and the authors of works on Wright whose published work, in the form of analysis, history, biographical detail, and architectural information proved particularly helpful (see full details in the bibliography), including Bruce Brooks Pfeiffer, Robert McCarter, Neil Levine, and William Allin Storrer. Dana-Thomas House images are reproduced by courtesy of the Illinois Historic Preservation Agency.

## CONTRIBUTORS

**Margo Stipe** is Registrar and Art Collections Administrator for the Frank Lloyd Wright Archives at Taliesin West in Scottsdale, Arizona. She is the author of *Frank Lloyd Wright, the Interactive Portfolio* (2004), and she plays a major role in the production of Frank Lloyd Wright Foundation publications and exhibitions. (Introduction)

**Jessica Hodge** is an author and editor whose credits include a wide range of publications over a thirty-year period in architecture and the arts, specializing in the arts of the twentieth century. She is from an Anglo-American literary family: her grandfather was the Pulitzer Prize-winning poet and novelist Conrad Aiken, and her mother and aunt were both prolific writers. She studied architectural history at Birkbeck, a college of the University of London, after receiving her Masters degree from the University of Oxford. (Chapters 3, 6, and 9)

**Robin Langley Sommer** is an author who has been writing books on architecture, design, and related historical subjects for more than three decades. She is the author of five previous works on Wright, four of which were collaborations with Balthazar Korab. (Chapters 7 and 8)

**Doreen Ehrlich** is an author whose previous books include four titles on Frank Lloyd Wright, primarily covering his early works, art glass, and interiors. (Chapters 1, 2, 4, and 5)

## PHOTOGRAPHY AND ILLUSTRATION CREDITS

**Balthazar Korab**, best known today as a distinguished architectural photographer, is himself an architect who has worked with some of the leading twentieth-century practitioners of the profession. He has won prestigious prizes for both his architectural and photographic work over the course of his long career, and is the author of several books on architecture. He received the American Institute of Architects' Lifetime Achievement Award for Photography in 2007, the same year in which the Hungarian Institute of Architects presented him with an honorary award for lifetime achievement.

**Christian Korab** is an artist, photographer, and specialist in digital mastering of photographs.

**Paul Rocheleau** is an acclaimed architectural photographer whose images have appeared in many prestigious publications.

The publisher also gratefully acknowledges the photographers for permission to reproduce their copyright images. All photographs are by **Balthazar Korab** except as noted:

© **Christian Korab:** 2, 7 (right), 11 (top left), 23, 24, 25 (top center), 26, 27, 30, 31 (right), 34 (top), 34–35, 36, 37 (top, bottom right), 38–39 (all; reproduced by courtesy of the Willits-Robinson Foundation), 48 (bottom), 50 (both), 58 (top), 59 (top), 61 (right), 118, 119 (bottom right), 162, 163, 164, 165 (both), 166; **Library of Congress, Historic American Buildings Survey/Historic American Engineering Record Collections:** 9 (top left, HABS ILL,16-OAKPA,5-, photographed by Philip Turner, 1967), 12 (three at top left, bottom left; HABS CAL,19-LOSAN,70-, Storer House drawings by Joseph R. Bateman, 1972; HABS CAL,19-LOSAN,62-, Freeman House block drawn by Robert C. Giebner, 1969; aerial isometric drawn by Jeffrey B. Lentz, 1969), 13 (two at top left, top right, two at bottom left; HABS VA,30-FALCH,2-, Loren Pope House drawn by James M. Hamill, 1964; HABS WIS,51-RACI,5-18, Johnson Wax interior photographed by Jack E. Boucher, 1969; HABS VA,30-FALCH,2-16, Loren Pope photograph; HABS PA,26-OHPY.V,1-89 and HABS PA,26-OHPY.V,1-81, Fallingwater photographed by Jack E. Boucher, 1985), 14 (bottom left, HABS WIS,51-RACI,5-6, photographed by Jack E. Boucher, 1969); **Library of Congress, Prints & Photographs Division** 9 (top right), 10 (top center), 12 (top right), 15 (top center); © **Photo SCALA, Florence/© 2008 Frank Lloyd Wright Foundation, Scottsdale, AZ/Artists Rights Society (ARS), NY:** 67 (bottom), 104–105 (top), 120–121, 139 (bottom), 158; © **Paul Rocheleau:** 16–17, 32–33, 45, 56–57, 62 (top), 63, 79, 90, 91, 92, 99 (top), 116, 119 (two at top left), 122, 124–125, 128, 130, 131, 132, 133; © **Saraband, illustrator Deborah White:** decorative artwork 9–15, floor plans 25, 42, 53, 72, 87, 119, 141; © **Saraband Image Library:** 8 (top), 11 (two at top right, bottom right), 12 (top center, two at middle center), 15 (three at top left, bottom left), 72 (top, bottom right); **The Solomon R. Guggenheim Museum, New York. Photographs by David Heald © The Solomon R. Guggenheim Foundation, New York:** 154–155, 156–157, 160; **Installation view of *From Picasso to Pollock: Classics of Modern Art,* Solomon R. Guggenheim Museum, New York, July 4–September 28, 2003. Photograph by David Heald © The Solomon R. Guggenheim Foundation, New York:** 159.